The Journey
of the
Colorful Stars

A Pathway toward Love, Faith, and Healing

I0087264

Laura O'Neale

Published by Your Light Within LLC

Cover design by Laura O'Neale and Ion (John)
Dragutescu

ISBN 978-0-578-08310-0

Published in the United States of America
by **Your Light Within LLC**

Will be also translated into Romanian and published in
Romania.

With eternal love, *The Journey of the Colorful Stars* is dedicated to my first spiritual teacher, my grandmother Roza, and to my first esoteric teacher, Alexandru E. Russu, who taught me, guided me, and protected me on my spiritual journey while on earth, and thereafter from the spirit world.

Acknowledgments

I acknowledge from the bottom of my heart everyone in my life—my grandparents, parents, relatives, spiritual teachers, coaches, coworkers, friends, students, and spiritual partners—who have contributed to my happiness, growth, and learning process directly and indirectly, through sharing their love, teachings, support, requests for support, inspiration, and more. Love is the source of life, and needs to be acknowledged, nurtured, and shared. Be blessed through eternity.

With love and gratitude, I give special thanks to:
My esoteric teacher, for divine inspiration and guidance
Rod Terry, for book structure corrections and valuable insights
Whitney Harrelson, for editing and valuable insights
Hugh O'Neale, for valuable insights and, especially, for being an amazing spiritual partner and true source of love
My parents, Lidia Paduraru and Mirela Costea, for reminding me to share the most joyful moments of my life
Shahryar Fahimi, for valuable insights
Ion (John) Bogdan Dragutescu, for cover design.

I would like to give special thanks to Jill Ronsley (Sun Editing & Book Design) for editing my book.

Content

Introduction

We are mirrors for each other. We can find ourselves in each other, because at the core of our being, we are all *one*. I believe in myself, and therefore, I believe in you. I love myself, and therefore, I love you. I am a stand for my shining light, and therefore, I am a stand for your shining light, too.

Our pathways might be different; however, the same light of inspiration leads us forward. A very important part of my spiritual mission is to share my life story, with its struggles, interpretations, lessons learned, sources of healing, and teachings. They all led me toward finding myself, reconnecting with my spiritual essence, and becoming a happy and peaceful soul.

The idea of writing *The Journey of the Colorful Stars* was born toward the end of 2006, in a moment of inspiration and profound feeling of gratefulness I had for my first esoteric teacher, Alexandru E. Russu, who had passed away about twelve years previously. His teachings had been sustaining me in many ways along my spiritual path, and therefore, I wanted to honor him in return through the eternal life a book provides.

When I was catching up with my past experiences and writing about my esoteric teacher, my channel of communication with him opened fully; from the spirit world, he "picked up the call," and started to lead my steps towards a new life, one that was aligned with the Source of all things.

—

This created a snowball effect of meaningful spiritual experiences that wanted to be shared, and I, thus, started to see the shape of this book.

Ever since, I've been writing at the end of each day about every little observation I had that pertained to my spiritual journey, every single thing that made my heart sing. It wasn't only about my first esoteric teacher anymore; it was about everyone in my life, for everyone is my teacher.

The title of *The Journey of the Colorful Stars*, my first book, was inspired by a life-transforming dream that I had around the age of nineteen. The dream was a revelation of my pathway toward faith healing, and stepping into Oneness with the divine light.

The Journey of the Colorful Stars explains that every life circumstance and experience, good or bad, is meant to help us pay our karmic debts, learn important lessons that our soul chose to address during this lifetime, and, ultimately, find our soul mission.

We have to remove barriers so that our vision about life aligns with our spiritual essence. Then, we remember who we are and what we came here for. Sharing my own life experience as an example of this required me to be *real*, and I opened up completely. There was no way for me to talk about a few things I reveal in this book before I had healed myself from deep emotional traumas. It would have triggered too much pain. In the end, it was very fulfilling and I am now offering hope: we can all heal ourselves.

A summary of the first 33 years of my life, this book depicts a progressive spiritual awakening and gives transformational, universal tools that we can all use. One by one, my life experience reveals how I got to the universal understandings presented in the first chapter, "Diamonds of Light for a Happy Life."

I am inviting you to read this book with an open heart and mind, and let it inspire you to find your teacher, your power within, and your own spiritual mission. In the process, remember, you are not alone: the colorful stars are here for everyone.

The description of my spiritual journey does not end with *The Journey of the Colorful Stars*; it is continued instead through other books, which are more specialized in particular subjects, such as reiki healing, shamanic practices, sacred love, and more.

With much love and joy, I invite you to let *The Journey of the Colorful Stars* be a mirror for your soul and help you find your light within. Enjoy.

Diamonds of Light for a Happy Life

The greatest power in the universe is the power of love from which God created us.

Where there is God, there is peace.

Always thank God; the Creator is at the heart of everything.

Nobody can take God from us; if we believe in God, we are blessed. God isn't hard to know, God is right here.

The healing power, imagined as colorful stars, will flow through faith.

Nature teaches us about harmony, about abundance, about union with the Divine; it doesn't matter how long the winter is—in the spring, we realize that nothing has died, and we can grasp with amazement the beauty of revival.

Thoughts, emotions and feelings are not a joke. They attract and create things matching their vibration. True happiness on earth is to live a life of unconditional love; by doing so, the soul is automatically liberated from attachments.

We are never alone; we always have spiritual guides around us. Before we choose and learn to consciously follow our spiritual guidance, it is given to us during sleep. Sometimes we remember, and sometimes we don't, but it's always available to us.

We can heal through love.

Where love and acceptance are present, responsibility is joyful and empowering.

All blessings of life come with homework. Unless we learn to embrace the whole package of our life experience we're missing out on the most delightful part—learning the lessons, opening our hearts, growing spiritually.

True light and faith are inside of us.

Constant empowering self-talk is a great tool for pulling ourselves back up. Yes, we can! It's our choice! Life is beautiful!

Become! Be *the flowing fountain of life-giving water.*

When we say "I'm alone," we disregard God and our guardian angels that are always with us.

We have a solid connection to God's love, through self-love.

We can only respect and love ourselves when we respect and love our parents. They are also a metaphor for our Mother Earth and our Father God.

The experiences, circumstances, and people in our lives are helping us pay our karmic debts, learn our lessons, and ultimately, accomplish our soul mission. When we finally understand, accept and start following our soul mission, we find bliss in our hearts.

We can avoid future karmic debt by learning the lessons that are presented to us by life.

I am reborn through my love for you, to a new life, given to God.

I can claim any spiritual gifts; the miracle is already inside of me, and so it is in everyone.

We don't need to know everything, but we need to have faith, and let love lead our way.

We all need to help ourselves first. And by doing so we automatically help others, too—simply because we are all one.

When we truly connect with the Divine within, we can forgive ourselves and others.

Discipline helps us become as powerful as we can be. Prayer, meditation, affirmations, and visualization are excellent disciplines.

Being grateful for our blessings is all God asks in order to give us more.

Our journey leads us toward remembering our destiny.

Imagination is a powerful magnet. The law of attraction reveals that as we align with our higher self, our dreams are aligned with our destiny. We dream and we might think that we create something new, but in fact we just make room for our destiny to unfold.

It's very important that we live what we learn. Reading books is helpful and inspiring, but it is not enough. We have to live the truth of our soul, to incorporate each new element into all areas of our life.

Forgiveness, the experience of love versus fear, builds self-esteem and self-love.

In any relationship, there is a choice we need to make between fear and love.

Loving relationships are the key, the most powerful tool of enlightenment.

Unconditional love means loving everyone regardless of one's condition, actions, or beliefs. It comes with the understanding that we are all part of a whole. It starts from within, from self-love and self-acceptance.

Becoming creatures of unconditional love, we experience heaven in our hearts, in the now!

Spiritual awakening and transformation takes time; patience is a virtue we need to cultivate.

We are all blessed and gifted and we need to maintain these blessings and gifts. We eat and drink water to maintain life. We work out to be in shape. We nurture our loving relationships to keep the butterflies. To awaken spiritually, to maintain and expand our spiritual gifts, we need to meditate, keep our hearts opened, and allow the power of love to unfold into our lives.

We all have the seeds of being everything—from the lowest to the highest being that ever walked on earth; however, what we feed determines which part of us manifests in the world.

By inviting divine guidance, we choose freedom from the fear generated by not being able to control.

Our number one guardian angel is our pure heart. In our daily life, as well as in our astral traveling, we attract things and entities that are in harmony with our vibration.

It is essential that we stay focused on light.

Childhood and Teenage Years

My grandmother Roza—a candle in the world

My grandmother Roza's faith and wisdom fascinated me throughout my childhood. Later in life, I understood that she was my first spiritual teacher. She was a wonderful storyteller, a woman of incredible courage and dignity, who had neither fear of life's challenges nor fear of death, but only love and light in her heart.

She used to start her day with a prayer. During the day, she would take little breaks for prayers. At night, she would go to sleep only after she had thanked God for all the blessings and lessons of the day, and she would say a prayer again.

Always thank God; the Creator is at the heart of everything.

Almost every summer, Roza would take me with her to resorts or on trips across Romania, the country where I was born, or to visit her brother, Gheorghe. I was always very moved and inspired by her conversations with him, and with everyone else who crossed her path. My time spent with her was always filled with joy, teachings, and wonder. She wasn't just my protective and caring grandmother, she was my best friend.

Nobody can take God from you; if you believe in God, you will be blessed. God isn't hard to know, God is right here.

During Communism in Romania, spirituality was not in harmony with the law. However, Roza helped so many people keep their faith, by taking the risk of being an ambassador of Divine Love, and talking to people about the soul, about eternal life, about forgiveness, love, healing, Jesus, and God.

The Communists—what do they know? They can't get rid of God just because they outlawed Him. God cannot be dismissed.

She was talking with people about Jesus' love, healing, and teachings. As a child, I wasn't necessarily religious, but rather fascinated by the miracles Jesus performed and thought about Him as being the most powerful healer of body, mind, and spirit. Jesus became my idol, just like movie stars are idols for other kids. Therefore, I used to spend a huge amount of time imagining how I would place my hands on people and see them being instantly healed from whatever disease they might have had. *My greatest desire was to be a healer.*

Roza crossed over when I was fourteen. Three days in advance, she knew the exact day, hour, and minute that she was going to take her journey to the other side. Twenty minutes before she closed her eyes, she said, *I see the light.*

—

I wasn't there when that happened, but when, later that day, I saw the incredibly blissful smile on her breathless face, I understood the power of her faith, and believed in its truthfulness more than ever. I felt happy for her, knowing that she went to a place filled with light, peace, and infinite love.

For many years, every once in a while, I had dreams about her coming back home. In the dreams, I never knew she had passed away and used to ask her, "Where have you been all this time? Were you sick? Were you in a hospital? Did you move?" She never answered. Only later in life, when I finally accepted her death at the subconscious level, these dreams stopped forever.

———

My mom—messenger for miracles

My mom has been suffering from a disease that has no cure. I was deeply affected by that in many ways throughout my childhood, and wished that a miracle would happen to heal her. How could I have not believed in miracles, knowing that she could have given up having children to protect her wellbeing? She was given one chance in a million of survival through pregnancy and birth if she chose to have a child. My existence on earth, therefore, was only through a miracle.

I love my mom, and always saw the incredible purity of her heart as being the source of her survival. When I was young, she used to come and pray over me every night before falling asleep, touching my face with her soft, light hands, like a feather....

Years later, I understood the importance of those few minutes, spent together in such spiritual communion. I knew that this is what I wish for any child—to go to sleep loved and surrounded by angels.

My mom was very amused and refreshed by my laughter, and very inspired by my blue eyes. As a poet, she wrote, through the years, a few poems about my eyes—poems that touched my soul.

Have I ever been the grass around the blue wild flowers?
Blue like my daughter's eyes?

The little girl

... I'm watching her getting closer
With her hair in the wind

I'm kissing her eyes
Crying
And I encourage her to step further with faith
Over the waves of the sea, beyond the horizons
And when she'll reach the zenith
I'll ask her to send me back the childhood
Surrounded in smiles, surrounded by purple rain....

—Mira Parang, poet

My father—an example of commitment, patience, and strength

For many years, my father led a large number of people in his workplace, and they loved and appreciated him very much.
He was so patient and understanding. He knew how to motivate them, help them, and correct them when necessary. Sometimes he had to work very late, and I remember how, in my bed, I would imagine my own sadness and sorrow in the event of an accident; but he would come back safe every time. He knew how to protect himself in the event of a fire or other industrial accidents.

While I was still in elementary school, he took me once with him to the huge industrial enterprise where he worked. He showed me the big difference that existed between those who had an education and those who didn't, in terms of the complexity of their work and the comfort levels they had while working.
Then, he asked me to think about it, and choose how I wanted to spend my life.

—

Even though I've seen my father crying only a few times in my life, one day he told me with tears in his eyes that he wished I would become a doctor and discover a treatment for my mom. I loved my father deeply and his tears impressed me so much. I will never forget that day. However, I had no calling to study medicine. Instead, Jesus' healing hands were the stars of my sky. My wish was to just place my hands on my mom and see a miracle happen.

In Romania, however, during Communism there were no healing arts schools or certified healers. Therefore, it seemed that becoming a healer was a fantasy.

My grandmother Mama Nana—a messenger of ancient healing arts

Every summer, I spent at least a month at my other grandmother's house in the village. She was a very honest, hard-working woman who loved animals, nature, and God in a very profound way. She taught me to have a great work ethic. I also did a lot of cooking, gardening, farming, and housekeeping with her. She cooked all kinds of delicious traditional foods for me, and showed me her love in so many ways.

When I was about to catch a cold, she would prevent it from happening by giving me massages, putting my feet in hot water with salt, and giving me a big cup of hot goat's milk before going to bed.
 As a result, while at her house, I was never sick.

—

24

My joy with animals and nature

Having no siblings to play with, I used to spend hours every day playing with animals, observing their behavior and their language. Everyone thought I would become a veterinarian. Every spring break, Mama Nana used to bring me a hat filled with little chickens (just coming out their eggs), asking me to take care of them and feed them from my palm with corn meal. What joy! Years went by, but I've never felt the revival of the spring so powerfully.

My dog was an incredible loving and devoted friend. The whole village would know when I was coming back. She would run from the back of the yard, filled with joy and excitement, and jump into my arms, play, and fill my heart with so much happiness. We would communicate telepathically: I would imagine how she should help me chase the chickens out the garden, and she'd do exactly that. One night, all of a sudden, I felt an irrational impulse to go outside and take a look in the yard—I found her just in time to save her from dying. She had wanted to jump over the fence, and her chain had got stuck between two pieces of wood. She was hanging on the fence, not even yelping, but she had silently called for me. Her gratitude was immense. Years later, while studying telepathy, I wondered how in the world I had known how to practice it with my dog.

Nature was also a source of joy and amazement for me. I used to look for colorful stones in the sand, a passion carried through the generations (my parents studied mineralogy, geology, and petrography at the Institute of Mines in Petrosani).

I used to look at any plant, tree, or flower with a big smile on my face. Both Mama Nana and my father planted many flowers that transformed the garden every spring into a little paradise. Throughout the years, I told them many times that these wonderful flowers represented a mirror of their soul.

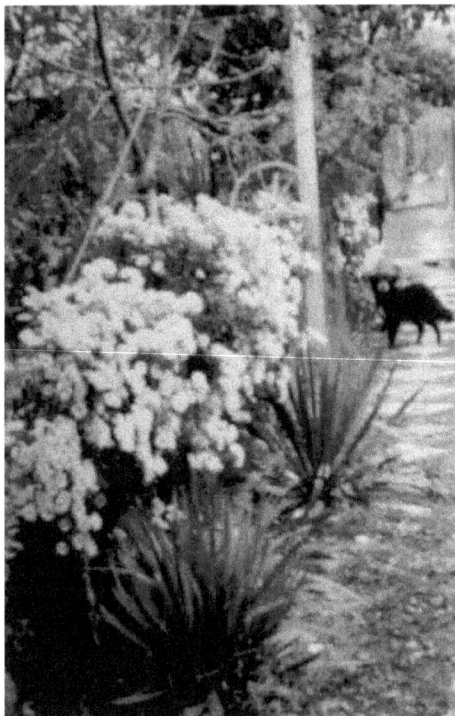

Sometimes I spent hours imagining that I was merged with nature—that I was the grass, or the wind, or the tree—and that gave me pure joy.

Many times I would refuse to take naps in the house after lunch, but rather outdoors, on a little bench in the garden, surrounded by trees, plants, and flowers, enjoying the sun and the birds—with the baby ducks and chickens running around. Mama Nana couldn't make me wear shoes the whole summer. I loved feeling the dirt, the grass, the mud … the earth, under my feet.

If we love the trees, the rocks, the birds and animals and all things as the Infinite made them, shall they not in response to our love give us each of their peculiar thought and wisdom? Shall we not draw nearer to God through a love for these expressions of God?
—Prentice Mulford

My childhood dreams—bridges between past and future

Throughout my childhood and teenage years, I had some extraordinary dreams. Pretty often, I dreamed that in Mama Nana's house, under my favorite room, was a hidden room, like a secret basement, in which was kept a treasure. I dreamed that so many times, but only later in life, reading the book *Reflections, Dreams and Memories* by C.G. Jung, did I understand that the hidden room represents the subconscious mind. The interpretation of my dream helped me believe in myself more: "I didn't discover it yet, but I knew that my power within was waiting to be unveiled."

Many times I dreamed that I was flying. Sometimes I couldn't fly high enough so that people were able to drag me down by my feet.

My body was heavy, and flying was similar to swimming. Sometimes I dreamed that I was flying over buildings, including one of the buildings in Washington, DC, which I was shocked to see about fifteen years later while coming back from lunch.

There is always one moment in childhood when the door opens and lets the future in.
—Deepak Chopra

When I had that dream, I was in Romania and had never been in DC. I still felt my body, and the effort needed to fly was huge and challenging. But once, I dreamed that I was flying higher and higher, until I felt no body at all. I experienced total peace, total silence, and total emptiness. It was so unique and powerful! I came down to the ground after a while, and I felt my body again, and my feet touching the ground. That dream made me want to explore the spirit world as never before.

At times, I dreamed an ocean was hidden under the ground, and the feeling associated with that dream was *infinite power*.

A few interesting dreams brought me memories from some of my previous lives, including five of my deaths in which I was killed. In the most "ancient" of those previous lives, I was a slave who died for the purpose of entertaining her masters. I was terrified of what I was asked to do, and knew that I would die. There were many others there, and one of them was a very close person, who looked at me in those moments, and through the love and the peace, and the wisdom in his eyes, instantly liberated me from the fear of death.

28

The moments following my liberation from fear, in which I was killed, were peaceful moments, were seconds of void. That could have been my first incarnation in which I died in peace—and that remained with me in future incarnations. I was never again afraid in other dreams reliving other life-ending moments, but rather perceived the moment of death as a jump toward a new dimension.

Years after the dream in which I was a slave, I recognized that close person as being my great friend Adrian.

My early challenge—a karmic tool

I remember a conversation that a dear aunt had with my grandmother Roza about the challenges of life. They couldn't believe when, interrupting their conversation, I told them that "I do not want to try to escape the challenges of life, but rather go out there in the world, have them soon and be done with them." To me, it was crystal clear that certain things *have* to happen. Obviously, I had no clue about the concept of *karma* at that time, but something in me knew that my challenges had to come, and only then I would start a new life. At that time, I was about thirteen.

Sure enough, I didn't have to wait long. Soon after Roza's death, I got to face my challenges, my karmic debts. Being lost for a while in the darkness of the soul, experiencing distrust, fear, self-doubt, inconsideration, threat, anger, guilt, numbness … you name it ... my soul almost wanted to escape my body.

In the circumstances, I had nothing left but God. Much later I understood that having nothing left but God was a "must have" experience in my awakening process.

You can start with nothing, and out of nothing and out of no way, a way will be made
—Rev. Dr. Michael Bernard Beckwith

On the edge between life and death, I was helped by God through a wonderful man, who saved my life, and more importantly, my soul. His name was Elton. I knew he would save me before I even saw him. Something made me look toward my right and wave my hand, asking that way for help. In an instant, I revived from the inside out, shifting from a state of emotional numbness and resentment, to a state of infinite hope, gratefulness, and joy. That was a very powerfully recognized *soul's reunion*—meeting someone with whom I had an agreement before I was born.

After all the shocking events that happened to me, I spent six months far away from home with my uncle Romica and aunt Viorica. The harmony and beauty of their life, the flowers in their garden, their understanding, their love and care, their children—my cousins, who were like brothers to me—as well as the new city, helped me during my emotional recovery.

All these experiences, some happy, some very painful, some very special, all very deep, made me want to study human nature even more, to understand and heal myself.

Everything in your life is there as a vehicle for your transformation. Use it!
—Ram Dass, spiritual teacher and author

—

A Life-Transforming Dream

When I was about eighteen years old, my mom sparked my interest in reading books about the unseen forces of the human mind. Communism was now over, and such books had just started to be available to the public. Through reading, I understood that my desire to heal was not just a fantasy and that there were people in the world that are using their greatest power within for the highest good of human kind. I was inspired to imagine that *the magic power of the universe exists all over space in the shape of billions of shiny little colorful stars.* I was inspired to imagine that in order for me to become a healer, I must learn how to attract the colorful stars, so that they would come together like a little spiral and surround me for protection, enter into my hands for healing, into my head for wisdom, and into my heart for the power of love.

Soon after imagining that, I had an amazing dream. I was in the middle of a green field. A white horse came to me. The horse had wings. Next, I was riding the horse, who soon began to fly, higher and higher, until we got into the deepest darkness I had ever seen. Then, I started to see the colorful stars, all over and around, to hear their sound and to feel their healing, protecting, and peaceful energy.

There were billions of colorful stars, and their beauty was more than I could have ever imagined. After a while, we came back down to the ground. Somehow, the white horse wasn't with me anymore. There was just an empty field, and in the middle of it, a huge cross.

Mama Nana was there, and it seemed that it was the time of her death. Looking at the sky, all of a sudden, I saw a huge spiral of colorful stars coming toward the ground, and entering into the cross.

Graphic design: John Dragutescu

I woke up energized, amazed and confused in the same time. I couldn't interpret my dream for many years, but when I did, it became clear to me that *the colorful stars will only come through faith.*

During the following summer, my mom asked me go with her and visit an old lady who she admired a lot. While visiting the woman, I had the most wonderful and unexpected surprise: the lady showed me pictures from her traveling, and one of them was a photo of an older man surrounded by three Indian yogis.

Instantly I felt the urge to know more about him. So she told me that she had known him since she was a child, at that time he was about twenty years old, and he was already known for being "the healer,"—the one who healed people by touching them, or simply giving them a glass of water to drink in which he had released energy from his fingers. His name was Alexandru E. Russu Bahmut.

I wanted to meet him right away. My calling was so overwhelming, I would have done anything to meet him. The lady did not want to give me his address, saying that he was now too old and didn't want to meet new clients or students anymore. My whole being knew, though, that it was meant to be ... there was no way for me to miss him.

My First Esoteric Teacher

Alexandru E. Russu opened the door while I was coming up the stairs. His spirit knew I was on my way, even though I had not announced my visit. Finally meeting him was so overwhelming. I was trembling like a leaf in the wind.

The most powerful person I had ever met had such an old, skinny, powerless body. He seemed so fragile that I burst into tears and hugged him. My heart was filled with compassion, pure love, admiration, and infinite hope. I trusted him fully in a fraction of a second. His energy was divine.

I asked him to teach me. Tears were falling down my face. It was the most profound desire of my life. I wanted to become like him, and be able to help myself, my mother, and everyone else. I wanted to be able to see and hear beyond my senses. I wanted him to be my teacher, and that desire itself was so profound, it felt like a remembrance of an old pact. He told me that nothing happens by chance, that he knew I would come and that he was supposed to teach me. It was meant to be.

When I sat down on a chair, I looked at his portrait on the wall, which was painted when he was about forty-five years old. His blue piercing eyes frightened me for a second, but then I knew that they were on my side, and that I was blessed to be there.

I could have been his great-granddaughter, so he called me "Fetito" or "fetita mea" ("little girl" or "my little one" in Romanian).

Speaking of teaching, he said that some people offered him huge amounts of money to teach them, but they never got a word out of his mouth because they were not supposed to find the teachings. "When you get to know yourself, you will know the will of God," he said. "In the meantime, don't tell anyone what I'm teaching you. You are an entity. You have *your own* universe in which nobody has to come." He also told me that everyone who is meant to learn will find a teacher when they are ready.

He spoke about the importance of quieting the mind, focusing on one thing at a time. *Learn to focus! When you master your mind, you'll master everything.* Then, he taught me a few meditation techniques. Learning to focus and getting in the habit of meditating daily were the foundation on which he could help me build a "temple." It was supposed to take time, just as babies need nine months to be born.

At one point, he led me to his guest room and gave me a big stack of typed notes from his journal to read overnight. I didn't close my eyes the whole night. It was absolutely incredible. His awakening, his development, his healing cases, his travels around the world, everything would have been incredibly powerful even as a science fiction book. His intention was to publish a book, since Communism was now over, but he unfortunately didn't get a chance before he took the journey to the spirit world.

The next day, as we walked together through the park for almost two hours, we talked about what I had read in his journal. He told me even more amazing things about his healing cases, his hypnosis sessions, his astral journeys, his life experiences, and about his past lives.

He told me to never forget that not by chance are we all human beings, in flesh and bones, and that I should never refuse the idea of enjoying earthly life. In other words, I should not just focus on spiritual development, but, rather, treat all aspects of my life as equally important.

When I left and hugged him again goodbye, I felt so blessed by God for having met him. On my way back home, I realized that I was not the same. For the first time in my life, being a healer was not just a dream anymore. "Everything is possible!"

Notes from my teacher's journal

I wish to remember everything I read in his journal and share it with the whole world—as he would have done if he had had a chance before crossing to the other side. However, this is all that I can recall after so many years:

Alexandru E. Russu was born in Basarabia, in a small village. Around the age of eleven, his parents sent him away to school, where he lived in a dormitory with two other boys. At one point, one of the boys had a very intense stomach pain. My teacher looked at his roommate, and placed his hands on his stomach while sitting still.

After about twenty minutes, the pain was gone. My teacher's ongoing headache was gone, too, for the first time since he was born. He acted by instinct. Nobody had ever taught him what to do to heal someone.

This was the beginning of his magic life. Within a few months, he had become famous. People were waiting in line for days to get an appointment with the young, but very powerful healer. He started to discover the differences between people's illnesses in terms of how much energy and how many sessions he needed to give them.

Soon, it was Alexandru's time to meet his teachers. Somehow, he got into a secret German esoteric school where his natural abilities were studied and developed further. When he left the school, he already knew how to master his mind, how to manage his powers, how to use various hypnosis techniques, and how to sharpen his ability to see and interpret what he was able to see with the eye of his mind.

After three years of school, he went back to his hometown and started to practice healing again. He never stopped until he died at the age of ninety-one.

Throughout his life, he traveled all over the world, being invited by famous and powerful people to come and heal them of all kind of diseases. He was well known for being one of the most efficient natural healers of his time.

He developed relationships with a few doctors in the hope of finding the link between spiritual healing and the traditional medical approach.

—

Many of his notes were summarizing conversations with these doctors who were fascinated by his healing cases. However, during Communism it was impossible to talk freely about spiritual healing, and they couldn't go too far.

Alexandru was also working for the mental health hospital in Bucharest for a while. Some of his notes depicted cases of mentally ill patients who were almost impossible to help. He told me that serious mental illnesses were teaching him the limitations of his gift.

While he was in his forties, Alexandru spent a few years in India, where he had been telepathically called to visit by a master in yoga techniques. He developed his natural abilities even further, deepened his yoga practice, and later built a temple with his master.

At another point in his life, he spent six months completely alone in the heart of a forest. Someone brought him bread and water once a week and put it in a certain place for him. He rigorously exercised every day, eating only bread and drinking only water. After a few months of being alone in the woods, his senses strengthened to the point that he could hear from beginning to end a concert that was taking place two thousand miles away.

Alexandru connected with the Universal Consciousness while hiking on a mountain in France, and his whole view about life jumped to another stage.

He was traveling outside his body, consciously guiding his dreams. He knew about all his previous lives and was continuously connected with the spirit world.

—

Ironically, he was born without the sense of smell…. And when I met him, he was almost blind, but what fortune to have his third eye fully opened.

I was being seduced by the magical experiences

Alexandru told me to meditate fifteen to twenty minutes every day, no more than that. But as I got caught in the beauty produced by the meditation techniques, I wanted to do it more. I started to spend more and more time in the altered state of consciousness, sometimes over an hour. That wasn't a good idea, but at least at that time, my teacher was still alive, and I knew I was protected by him at all times, even though he lived far away.

In the beginning, whenever I meditated, I would start feeling dizzy, and not fully aware of my physical body. Sometimes the wall in front of me would look like it was pulsing, like a heart, then the image would start to rotate, forming a vortex. My lungs would fill with air. I felt as if rivers were flowing through my body, rivers of energy and peace. When I told my teacher about the vortex in the wall, he told me that this was the sign of starting to travel outside of my body and that I was not yet ready for that.

There is a time to let things happen and a time to make things happen.
—Hugh Prather, author, minister, and counselor

When I was learning how to meditate, I found the beginning of each session to be very difficult. After a while, I found I could reach a quiet and peaceful moment. I was tempted to not stop the meditation, for that peaceful moment couldn't be reached any other way. I was at least obedient enough, though, to stop for a few seconds every time the wall started to "move." My hands were burning with energy. I could feel the energy between my palms up to thirty inches.

Little by little, I started to love everything and everyone around me. I had more patience, and changed the nature of my concerns. I was another person.

In about four or five months, I started to see a pale light around my head and a shiny, bright light around my hands. They were warm and their shiny color was a mix of yellow, orange, and white. My fingers were almost transparent. I asked myself why I couldn't see my face in the same way. Sometimes I couldn't see my face at all, but saw two lights instead of my eyes.

While meditating, all my senses went somehow inward. My thoughts were increasingly leaving me alone until I would experience a profound state of peace. Deep in my heart, I knew that this meditation technique was the vehicle to reach a new dimension.

I wanted to be able to give everyone the gift of being able to see the light inside of him or her.
"I'll master my mind. I'll find myself, whatever will happen to me. I'll get back on track, stronger and more powerful than before."

—

I felt a powerful calling that made me unstoppable. It was such a strong, deep calling, I wanted to leave the earthly daily life, and be alone in the mountains for a while. I loved my maser so much but didn't listen to him—I was constantly going over the allowed time for meditation every day.

One day, my beloved friend Mirela had abdominal cramps. Her pain went away while I was keeping my hand on her painful spot. As she started to feel better, my hands were in bigger and bigger pain and heaviness. Almost twenty minutes were necessary for her pain to go away. Mirela and I use to meditate together, and that was my first experience of oneness in peace and joy. She believed in natural healing, and she believed in God.

Soon after that day, I dreamed that flashes of light were coming out of my palms and fingers.

I was fascinated by the power, and my ego took over. I was giving myself too much importance and underestimating others. I wanted to use the power of my eyes to impress and control people.

As a survivor of sexual abuse, blackmail, kidnap, and rape at an early age, I imagined how I would now defend myself against bad people or even taking revenge on them by using my power for the crimes they did to me in the past. So I extended my meditation time even more. When I did that though, I unbalanced my energy fields tremendously, which caused me to lose energy uncontrollably when I was surrounded by crowds of people. After a few months, my body started to retain water.

The doctor thought that was a sign of a very serious kidney disease, when in fact, years later I found that it was simply a symptom of exaggerated exposure to energy.

The next time I went to see my teacher he knew everything that I had done before I even started to tell him. He scolded me as if I was a little girl who was just learning to walk, and, excited by her new power, was running and falling down, hurting her knees. He told me not to open doors that I could not control. He also then told me to never practice the meditation techniques when I was sick. "Don't exaggerate. Don't do it more than ten to fifteen minutes at once. Everything has to happen step by step. Don't play with these unseen forces! Do only what I'm telling you to do."

Seeds planted in my heart

After that, I was a good student. I went back to visit him after a while, even though I wasn't ready for the next step. He answered all of my questions, though, and he continued to teach me new things.

For example, he taught me how to practice affirmations—a powerful lesson that I've used throughout my life.

When you bring forth a powerful thought form via affirmations and breathe/radiate that thought out into the world of form, you magnetize to you the elements needed to manifest that thought form in its material expression.
—Ronna Herman

43

On my way back home, I thought about moving to Bucharest were he lived, in order to be able to visit him all the time. I imagined myself taking good care of him, as he couldn't see anymore, and assisting him with his clients. I imagined myself typing up his handwritten journals and his healing cases, and helping him publish a book. I thought about learning from him faster ... there was so much to learn ... I thought about being more focused on my spiritual journey. However, for some reason, I didn't even call him for a long time, thinking that I hadn't got far enough to be ready for the next step that he would have taught me.

A few months later, someone told me that he had died. My whole world crashed around me within a second. The following day, I went to his house and knocked at his door for half an hour, crying, just to see and accept that, indeed, there was no one there to open the door anymore.

For a while, I refused to continue practicing his teachings. Being afraid, and also, stubborn, I refused to continue without him. I was attached to him, and loved him so much, with his old and dried but so peaceful hands, with his blue eyes that almost couldn't see anymore.... He was a miracle to me. As Jesus Christ is my way to God, he was my way to the miracle of healing. I realized that I had no reason to cry, since his soul was in an uncomfortable cage—his old and sick body. I also knew he wasn't afraid to die and that he knew that the soul is eternal. However, the feeling of loss affected me tremendously.

About six month later, I started my meditations again, being careful and obeying his teachings. After about six to eight months of balanced, peaceful, step-by-step growing, my heart filled with love and harmony. There came a time when my mom was very sick, but from inside, I found the necessary tools to deal well with the situation. I felt wiser and started to understand that real power is the power of love and peace. I was on my way toward my higher self.

I read many books on physiology, intuition, psychoanalysis, yoga, and other related subjects, eager to find more about the unseen forces of the human mind. I came to many understandings along the way about myself, my mom's state of health, and how I was going to live my life.

During this time, I loved the man in my life as never before. Everything was magic, but so new. Somehow it seemed hard to identify and recognize myself, and sometimes I didn't know how to live such a spiritual life. In such a context of love, I got pregnant, without conscious consent or desire. We were so afraid of having a baby that could carry over my mom's disease. We were still not mature enough to realize that judging God's will only brings pain. We were young and scared, and decided to not have the baby. After the abortion, though, I felt like a murderer. It was my spiritual suicide. "I killed love, and acted against my faith in God and against the harmony of my soul that I had just created."

As a result, I closed my heart and couldn't truly love for many years. That was the beginning of the end of our relationship, which finally ended ten years later. We paid for my mistake with years of unhappiness and confusion. I didn't practice the meditation techniques again for many years. I had to first forgive and heal myself, and learn many lessons along the way, before I was able to look again at myself in the mirror.

The Flame within Waits to Be Lit Again

Life kept unfolding. Without dedicating my life to my spiritual pathway, becoming a healer was still my deepest desire. I just wasn't ready for the manifestation of my soul's mission, and had to learn many important lessons first. While I didn't meditate daily, I never stopped reading books about the seen and unseen forces of the human mind.

Some of my favorite books were written by Carl Gustav Jung, Sigmund Freud, Mircea Eliade, Paul Brunton, and other less internationally known Romanian authors. My main interest was the understanding of human psychic ability, hypnosis techniques, paranormal phenomena, yoga, and the history of religious beliefs.

Knowledge is important, but not enough. Many wounds from the past were still in my heart. While at the core of my being I was very joyful, only certain people and the beauty of nature really helped me connect with my inner joy during those times.

***

Along the years, my friends John, Mirela, Bebe, Virgil, and Niki were my "Joy Spirits." They would make me laugh and feel free. We would see life as a game together. We would tell jokes, dance, be totally open and honest with each other, and accept each other totally with no doubt or judgment.

Going on vacation to the Black Sea, in the mountains, walking through the parks, by the river or simply taking a nap outside in the hay in Mama Nana's yard, always gave me lots of peace and joy.

My dear friend Lidia was my companion through my trips to all the amazingly beautiful parks in Bucharest. Her pure heart always called me to share with her the beauty of nature, to breathe in the fresh air, to feel that all was *well*.

Adrian, who loved camping and especially taking care of the fire camp, used to bring all his friends together every summer for days of joy, peace, and deep connection with nature. These days brought me my greatest joy for many years. I am so grateful to Adrian.

The fire is God.
The river is God.
The forest is God....
Yes, God, you are everywhere...
Peace is everywhere....
Could we just allow it in our hearts?

Nature teaches us about harmony, about abundance,
about union with the Divine; it doesn't matter how long
the winter is—in the spring, we realize that nothing has
died, and we can grasp with amazement the beauty of
revival.

***

At times, I had done healing on myself, but never thought
about doing that for reasons other than physical pain. My
beloved ones also experienced peace and healing coming
out my hands at difficult moments of their lives.

About two years after my teacher's death, my mom went
into the emergency room, in a profound coma. I arrived
there maybe six hours later. My father was sitting on a
chair near her in deep sorrow. Looking at each of them
with both compassion and sadness, I felt the urge to place
my right hand a few inches above my mom's forehead. I
prayed from all my heart and wished that God would use
me as a channel of energy and bring her back to
consciousness. A few minutes later, my mom revived.
She moved, and soon after, awoke. My father started to
cry.

Little by little, I realized that *love* is the key for my mission in life. However, a glimpse of truth is not enough. It is just the light at the other end of the tunnel. It takes time. Years went by.

After college, I moved to Bucharest and spent more time with my cousin Carmen, who is a psychologist and a very spiritual and cultivated person. She helped me keep alive my dream of becoming a healer through our long conversations, by lending me her amazing books to read, by practicing reiki and regression on me, and most importantly, by being an example. She also was a catalyst for me in moments of weakness when I would rather complain about my past than create my future. She helped me understand that thoughts are powerful and thoughts create. So I became more responsible about what I was giving my attention to.

My first interaction with the Cosmic Consciousness

It was in the middle of a long, lonely, and stressful winter. On one Saturday evening, I finally got together with a group of good friends to watch a movie on TV. The leading actress's role was one of a woman who had just come out of jail. She used to have very few moral values. That day, however, she ran into a boy whose parents had just been killed, and a calling to give started to shine in her heart. She took custody of this young boy, and by opening her heart, by giving and loving, she became who she really was—a wonderful, loving, fulfilled, and happy woman.

—

The movie engaged me emotionally with authentic feelings of pure love. All of a sudden, dizziness took me over. It seemed like a door opened to a different world, a different dimension. I found ease in my heart, and my thoughts were running faster than ever before. They were extremely clear.

Everything was in harmony and peace: thoughts, feelings, and sensations. I had profound love in my heart for everyone. I felt whole, perfect, and complete, and tuned in with the Truth.

In the astral plane, a shiny light was coming out my chest and stomach, and my palms were full of energy. I didn't see anything out of the ordinary, but experienced the true fulfillment, in an unexpected moment. I understood that the only way to get out of the darkness is from within, just like the actress in the movie that night.

That internal realization was so profound, I could have died in peace right then. I felt I was having an out-of-body experience, flying further and further away from my body.

While feeling my crown chakra opening wildly, I saw my grandmother and my dear friend Virgil (both had been in the spirit world). Then, Jesus Christ came to my mind, giving me so much peace.

In those moments, in the astral plane, I offered help to all my friends, and knew that it was my mission to do the same for many others who I hadn't met yet.

I told Jesus that he could take me if he wanted. I also truly understood the message of my grandmother's peaceful smile when she died. I also knew that the truthfulness of my experience was the revelation of my mission. It is the reason why I was to live: to help the ones who need help.

A feeling of being safe—not vulnerable anymore—allowed me to forgive. I knew that the truth is not something that can be offered as a gift, so I decided to let people look into my eyes and my heart, and see it if they're ready.

My body was very relaxed, out in space, and it felt good. I felt total peace, like never before, safe and secure, but aware that I would suffer again, aware that I would feel the pain and the human condition again.

For a long time, none of my beloved friends who were in the house disturbed me. It was meant to have this experience. I was whole, perfect, and complete. My smile was different from any other smile I ever had on my face. I received clear answers to all of the questions I asked myself at the time.

I wished I had been able to capture on paper all the thoughts that crossed my mind that night. I couldn't, but knew that even if I forgot them, I would remember them when I most needed to access this fabulous power within.

Five years later, when I was reviewing my notes from my teacher's journal, it occurred to me that I was in touch with the universal, Cosmic Consciousness. I realized that my experience was similar to his, but much less intense.

The energy of this wonderful experience gave me enough power to endure my father's accident a week later, and my hard time alone in the hospital three weeks later. Since then, my perception about people and things has changed. My intuition basically took off.
I started to see the truth hidden behind certain people's words, beliefs, and excuses, and other people's pure hearts hidden behind their fears.

Attachments are the slavery of the soul

Geny, one of my dearest friends, talked a lot about attachments as being the main source of suffering. We both read a book explaining the consequences of being attached, and how these invisible cords we create between ourselves and different things and people last through lifetimes. Detachment, regeneration, and rebirth were still big dilemmas for me. So, even though these concepts were making sense to me, I had a lot of resistance to letting go.

Until that point in my life, if I wanted something, I wouldn't give up the desire. If I was hurt, I would not forget, and so on. The main thing I would tell myself was "It is not fair," or "I deserve to have what I want."

It took me years to really reach the level of detachment necessary for my soul to be free. At that point though, as a result of our conversations, and in the given life circumstances, I was taught a lesson about attachments during sleep.

Being trapped in need, unfulfilled desires, and attachment, for a particular outcome, I went to sleep one night extremely tense. I had a very strange nightmare. In my dream, I got off the bed and went toward the window. There, I was trapped in a circle of negative unseen forces; my mind was clear, but I had no power to defend myself or act in any way.

Something was trying to push me to jump out the window, from the tenth floor, where I was living. There was a strange sound associated with the unseen forces, like a whiz, clack, or snap. It was coming from outside of me. I was in danger, weak, and vulnerable.

At some point, I heard a voice calling me in a heavy tone, "Fetito! Fetito!" Only my first esoteric teacher ever called me "Fetito" (little girl). It wasn't his voice, it seemed to be mine. It was him inside of me who called me until I woke up.

I opened my eyes but my dream continued in a way for a little bit. It seemed that I was still standing by the window, looking down, and I saw a big snake releasing my feet and going away.

I didn't know what to do. I didn't feel like getting off the bed, being afraid because everything was happening right there in the room. I didn't want to go back to sleep either, because everything was happening "there." So I felt trapped for a while. Then, I realized that being afraid to go back to sleep could generate insomnia in the future.

Ideas were crossing my mind at maximum speed. It was vital to bring back together all my power within. "Nobody can knock you down if you don't allow it." I was the one opening the gate to evil, through my weakness, through my so-needy nature that day.

That night I saw how bad it was to want something too much. Being attached by things creates a circle of negative energies entrapping one even more. During our astral traveling, these negative energies have even more power.

Years later, I read in a book that going to sleep in such mood would lead the spirit into places where the spirit meets negative non-physical entities.

During my sleep I was in danger, but the soul of my esoteric teacher, or the key that he left me, woke me up. I was allowed to see, with the eyes of my mind, the trap attracted by my own stubbornness in not letting go. Understanding that was a big relief.

That was a tough lesson on letting go of attachments.

Thoughts, emotions and feelings are not a joke. They attract and create things matching their vibration. True happiness on earth is to live a life of Unconditional Love; by doing so, the soul is automatically liberated from attachments.

The battle is within

For me, interpreting my dreams has been an invaluable tool for understanding teachings about the cosmic world.

In one of my dreams, I was in a room with two old women. One was good and the other one was bad. The bad woman was trying to take the good woman's soul. I was there, either witnessing their fight or being one or other of the old women.

At some point, seeing the good one in danger, I, the observer, gathered all my power together and looking in her eyes, I told her:

The greatest power in the universe is the power of Love from which God created us!

I said that so loud and clear, it woke me up.

Faith and magic powers bring peace within

In another dream, I recall being in a house full of negative energy. It seemed that there were rooms with people who were trapped and in pain, unable to leave the house. An evil spirit was there, but I couldn't see it. I knew that my grandmother was there, too. I knew that she wasn't able to walk because her bones were destroyed. I didn't feel powerful enough to confront the evil spirit so I went outside the house, and said: "God will give me thunderbolts."

Soon after this thought, I started to fly toward the clouds. The first thunderbolt came toward me and penetrated my chest, shaking my whole body. I felt an enormous power, something that I have never experienced before in my life. Then, a second thunderbolt came, not from the clouds, but from the Colorful Stars. The power was beyond words. It was the power of total peace within. I came down to the ground and went back inside the house. With all my senses inward, I went straight to my grandmother and I took her in my arms out of the house. I went with her to the forest and tied her with a rope around a tree. Then I told her: "*You'll come back on your own feet, because you have the key that you gave me (faith in God).*" Then I went back into the house. *I had no reason to fight. Having total peace within, I didn't summon any violence.*
The evil was gone. There was nothing within me anymore to bring the dark energies to life.

Years later, while studying the spiritual cause of diseases, I realized that the weak legs of my grandmother represented my own fear of the future. Her message, the strength of her faith, was the key to unlocking the doors during the unfolding of my soul mission.

The full moon's magnetic energy

For almost a year, I used to meditate on the full moon for ten to fifteen minutes every month, and felt its amazing and magic powers. For a while, I had dreams about the full moon coming to me and giving me light.

Sometimes I would dream that the moon was in my yard, as big as the house. The blinders would shake from the highly intense vibrations the moon gave off. Sometimes I would dream that the moon was beaming light and power at me, and sometimes I would pass out from being exposed to such an enormous amount of power. Every time was overwhelming and fascinating.

Moon meditation

Later, I understood that my spiritual guides taught me while asleep, and also helped me charge my energy fields.

We are never alone; we always have spiritual guides around us. Before we choose and learn to consciously follow our spiritual guidance, it is given to us during sleep. Sometimes we remember, and sometimes we don't, but it's always available to us.

———

Overcoming Steep Barriers

A new world

For seven years in a row, I applied to the Green Card Lottery, hoping to win and fulfill my dream of living in America. In 2003, my husband at the time and I won together and finally went to the United States. Even though it was hard to leave my wonderful parents and friends behind, my calling was pushing me forward. "Is it my destiny? Perhaps yes." Nothing happens by chance. It felt very natural for me to move to the U.S. However, it took me a few years to go through the basics of living life there, such as learning English, making a living, making new friends, and so on.

Shortly after I arrived in the U.S., it occurred to me that one could live in the "land of promises" and still be unfulfilled, poor, unhappy, sick, or lonely. It's not enough to live in America to make dreams come true. It is a country of all possibilities, good and bad, which means that it's up to each of us to make a good life. With that understanding in mind, for the first time in my life, I started to do my best by all means. I was grateful, self-determined, unstoppable, and free.

Heaven on Earth is a choice you must make, not a place you must find.
—Wayne Dyer, American self-help advocate, author, and lecturer

———

Two days after my arrival, I started to work in a Greek family restaurant. When you don't know the language and have no money to sustain yourself, you can't stay home and wait for the job of your dreams. It seemed a challenge but actually it was a wonderful opportunity to learn English faster, meet amazing people who became a second family for me, and live my first experience of oneness with people from other countries.

One of the owners was a wonderful man named Niko. I will never forget Niko. He is a real role model for any new immigrant trying to make it. My English was so poor, and in the beginning I made so many mistakes, it embarrassed me a lot. I apologized, but he said, "It's okay, Lorry, we all make mistakes in the beginning. You will learn. Only if you don't want to, you will not." He called me Lorry, which was the name of one of his daughters, who was born just a few days apart from me.

He told me his story, about his hard work in United States. He said, "Do you think I left my beautiful country to come here and stay poor?" Indeed, he made his dreams come true. He worked hard, honestly, laughing every day, helping everyone, and being a source of joy and peace. Meanwhile, he became very wealthy. He honored himself, his family, and everyone who came his way. I was so grateful and honored to work for Niko.

At some point though I found a job that fit my education and with tears falling down my face I announced to Niko that I had to leave and pursue my career. He congratulated me with so much joy in his eyes and said, "Don't cry, Lorry, you won't miss us, because you'll be here every Friday and Saturday night."

Without even asking him, he offered me the best night shifts as a part-time job.

I met so many other wonderful people, and some of them became friends for life. One thing to mention is that my heart was searching first for friends who played a parental role for me. Niko was like a father for me, and so was Roger.

Roger was my guardian angel, sent by God to guide me and protect me in the beginning of my new journey. He encouraged me so much during that time. He shared the story of his life with me, he picked me up and dropped me off before and after work, he cooked special meals for me, and helped me drive on the highway, as I was so afraid to do so in the beginning.

Eftihia could have been my aunt. We were always busy, always running, always laughing, always making our customers' day. She is a light in the world just by being who she is—a source of joy and unconditional, pure love.

People with golden hearts—pure, loving, and genuine—and who were born in different parts of the world have resonated with my soul so much.

The first people I met when I arrived in Washington, DC were from Greece, El Salvador, and Cyprus. They made my dream of seeing the *oneness that exists around the world* come true. These individuals created a strong foundation of trust, harmony, and love in my heart. This helped me explore my new world and expand my friendships further, transcending cultural and ethnic differences.

Called by ancestors?

Living in America felt like coming back home. I also found I was especially intrigued by the Native American and African-American cultures. They spoke to my heart and called me to explore myself more.

One of my biggest dreams was to meet a Native American Shaman. In my imagination, the Native Shaman would have become my new esoteric teacher.

After reading books about Native American shamans and chiefs, one day it occurred to me that my grandmother Roza's features were actually very similar to Native Americans'. It made me wonder was she a Native American in a past life, and did she carry with her the wisdom and features of those people?

*Similarities between Roza and
Native American Chief Hollow Horn Bear (Brule Lakota)*

I went to many powwows and did a lot of research on Native American medicine men.

One of my most special memories is from 2004 when the National Museum of the American Indian opened in Washington, DC. I spent a whole day on the National Mall, celebrating and meeting so many Native Americans. Some wore traditional costumes, and some were dressed in modern clothes. The whole experience caused tears of joy to fall down my face. A feeling of being back home surrounded me and nourished me. Did I live in North America in a past life? I didn't know at that point, but it felt so real.

People in my heart

My early experiences in the U.S. convinced me that I wanted a job that would enable me to support diversity and celebrate the richness of different cultures. I was so pleased to get a job with an organization whose mission was to diversify the legal profession and prepare tomorrow's leaders. The organization provides free academic seminars to college students and law school students across the country. Traveling across the United States during the academic seminars gave me the opportunity to meet amazing people from all over the world. It helped me achieve one of the dearest dreams I had about living in America.

Everyone in the organization was so nice to me and very patient and understanding with my poor English. I was very grateful and wanted to do my best professionally. My coworkers became good friends of mine and made me feel right at home. Mutual trust became very soon a powerful foundation of our great work environment.

For me, the organization also provided a great opportunity to learn a lot about the African-American culture, which was one of my most important goals. I was amazed to find how much our personalities are alike and how many traditions and proverbs are alike between Romanians and African-Americans.

One day, my coworker and friend Rod gave me a draft of his book *Hope Chest* to read. From the first page, I was amazed to see how African-American and Romanian women had the same loving way of saving a fortune for their daughters: in a beautiful wooden hope chest....

| *Romanian hope chest* | *African-American hope chest* |

Working and getting to know my coworkers was even more than learning about the culture. It was an opportunity to give back. By serving diversity, I was giving back to Elton, the man who saved my life and my soul, when I was young. He was an African-American student studying in one of the most prestigious Romanian schools when we met.

Self-discovery

In an effort to learn English faster, I started to listen to books on CD. The first two I will never forget, since they had a great impact on me: *The Psychic Pathway* by Sonia Choquette and *The Higher Self* by Deepak Chopra. I wanted to be like the authors one day. They gave me so much hope. My dream of becoming a healer, teacher, and psychic became more real, just because of them being who they are. Yet, there were many wounds in my heart that were still hurting and holding me back. It was time for me to focus on breaking through my barriers.

For almost six months, I participated in various courses and programs, which had a tremendous positive impact on my self-healing and self-discovery. My husband at the time encouraged me to go, largely in the hope of making our relationship work. It seemed to be too late for that, but the programs gave us the tools to come to closure in a way that brought us peace and a new friendship and spiritual connection.

Love versus fear

In one of the programs, the instructor led us through a "fear exercise." The only thing I was able to imagine during this exercise was my chest opening up and letting go of a lot of junk. No one was around to scare me. The fear was inside of me, and during the exercise I was able to let it go.

Too many of us are not living our dreams because we are living our fears.

—Les Brown: motivational speaker

As the junk was getting out my chest, on the astral plane, light started to brighten, more and more. Just a little bit of junk was left inside. Fear comes only from within. The light was a metaphor for love.

Fear and love cannot live together in the same place.

I felt that deeply. I felt that I can heal through love.

So, with love in my heart, I called my parents and apologized for my misunderstandings and misinterpretations of them in the past, and told them that I loved them very much. The phone calls were short, but my parents were very happy to hear what I had to say. A week later, my mom opened up to me like never before, and I was able to help her heal a forty-year-old wound that had been in her heart. She also told me that after that phone call, my father said to her that if he died, then he would die in peace. How liberating!

It felt so good to hear that, and also to know that I really helped my mom. She told me that she had never felt as close to me as she did at that point.

Later on, I wrote two letters, one to each of my parents, for the purpose of letting go completely of the major obstacles I had created between my parents and myself throughout my life. I'm sharing these letters with you because they say a lot about the radical impact incomplete relationships with parents can have on one's life.

It's not easy to share these personal stories, and many people might never understand or agree with me sharing them. I'm doing this in the hope that, by reading this book from beginning to end, you'll ask yourself, "What would I possibly accomplish by removing the barriers that exist between me and my parents?" I am a support for your greatness. I found the courage to share. And I encourage you to do the same and liberate yourself.

Completion with my dear mom

"My dear mom, like never before, I am now so very happy that you are my mom. I acknowledge that since I was seven years old and saw you sick, I haven't really considered you my mom. I rather saw you as a little sister I had to be careful not to hurt. Many times I felt unfortunate not to have a healthy mom, like other kids, and afraid that you'd become a burden in my life, a tough destiny that would ruin my life. I was scared by your presence in moments of your illness when I was little, and I spent many nights imagining how I would run away from home.

"Later on, I spent even more time imagining how I'd have to take care of you, and how no man would be able to accept this situation in his life. I thought, I'll be condemned to be alone. Then, I was afraid that I'd give birth to kids who would inherit your illness. Life seemed really miserable.

"All these inconsiderate thoughts and emotions were based on fear, not on love. Now I understand that by being afraid, my love for you was suppressed. You are so wonderful, and deserve all the love in the world. You are perfect just the way you are.

"Now I'm giving up my need of having a protective mother, and all these stories of misery and fear, and commit to love you for the wonderful, pure hearted woman you really are. I offer you the support you need from the bottom of my heart. Also, now I acknowledge that you were actually a hero, a survivor, who chose to risk her life by bringing me to earth."

Accepting my mom's illness revived my willingness to stand by her. This was an essential step for me to then be able to stand by anybody else. I felt empowered by opening my heart and giving it all: "I am now a river of love and I am happy!

Forgive me. I love you. Thank you."

Where love and acceptance are present, responsibility is joyful and empowering.

Completion with my dear father

"My dear Daddy, you were my hero, my dear dad, my dear friend.... I loved you so much all the time! But as many teenagers do, one day I became a rebel who wanted independence more than anything else.

You sensed that and told me that if I'm not listening to you, and not honoring our family's good reputation in your terms and in the community's terms, you will not consider me your child anymore. As you did that, I didn't trust you anymore. My whole world crashed around me, and I felt betrayed in my unconditional love for you.

"Now I know that you were only trying to scare me so I would stay away from trouble. At that time though, I accused you of betraying me for so many years. I now understand that it was not your pride or good reputation, but your fear that was speaking to me.

"You knew so well what kind of people were in our town—a place filled with communist mafia, well protected by the authorities and eager to take advantage of anyone coming their way. You knew that I was on the loop since I was a kid, simply by being your daughter— the child of a good and powerful man who stood for justice, and who had many enemies. I was only fifteen years old. As a result of our conversation, I felt I didn't have your support, and this was not too long after my grandmother died.

"Whose interpretation was that? *Mine!* You always loved me so much! As a result of not trusting you, though, in my mind, I was all alone. Acting as if nothing could be worse than facing you, I got into huge trouble. Not listening to you, my father, I trusted a schoolmate and went to visit a 'good friend' of his. Once there, I was sexually abused. Then, I was told that everyone in the school would know what 'I did' if I did not come back by myself. I was more than embarrassed, and wanted to hide underground so nobody would see me anymore.

———

He showed up at school threatening me. He called me at home, threatening me. I was such a silly youth, and did not see any way out of it. So I went back. Next, I was told that you would find out what 'I did' if did not play his game. He took me with him, far away from home, and things went even further into the darkness. I lost my humanity for a few days, and didn't care about myself anymore. I was physically alive, but my soul seemed to have left.

"Soon though, something miraculous happened— someone stood up for me and took me out of the hands of the criminal. His name was Elton. He saved my soul and probably my life, too. I knew he'd do that in the first second I saw him. In fact, my hope revived miraculously when I looked at him.

"He picked me up from the swamp, putting himself in danger. I cried in his arms for hours. His loving care helped me heal and revive. He was God to me. Tears fell down my face ... but that meant being 'alive' again.

"Meanwhile, you went through hell to find and save me. When things calmed down, seeing that you loved me and you were not the tough man of my imagination, I was sorry. However, I was still mad and for many years considered that you said those things to me because you were too proud.

"Luckily, all that misery and pain ended without causing unsolvable damage. I've learned a lot of things, and wanted to heal myself. I started to search and read, understand, and follow my soul mission early in life. I didn't die, but instead, I got much stronger.

—

"Now I know how much you always loved me, Daddy, and I ask you for forgiveness. I offer you all my love.

"Forgive me. I love you. Thank you."

Coming to peace with my father, I felt peace with everybody else, and, more importantly, with Our Father (a way of naming God) and His guidance.

***

I love you mother
I love you father
I love you daughter

After love and respect for parents comes respect and love of self. Forgive me. I love you. Thank you.

I can breathe again

Looking at my past from a new perspective, it occurred to me that what I had made things mean before was in total harmony with my *ego*.

Now I know what were the major barriers in the manifestation of my soul-mission: not fully accepting and loving, being resentful, being afraid, not trusting, acting on my own, refusing help as a result of being afraid. How could someone be a healer without being filled with love, acceptance and trust, and therefore, without accepting divine guidance?

Now I felt that I could breathe again ...

—

I could laugh again …
I feel free … and light like a feather
And filled with hope for a happy and fulfilling life,
Because I've learned my lessons,
Because I am at peace with my beloved family,
And so it's sunshine in my heart!

My question was how many millions of people have been making things mean something else than what they were? How many millions of people would feel relieved, free, happy, full of life and joy, if they could simply take a look within and accept to reconsider, to forgive themselves and love themselves, and to be at peace with everyone in their lives?

We can only respect and love ourselves when we respect and love our parents. They are also a metaphor for our Mother Earth and our Father God.

We can learn many things from other people's experiences. However, I noticed that the most important lessons for us, perhaps the ones our spirit chose to learn in this life, can best be learned through our personal experiences. Why? Because not just the mind has to learn, but the entire system: body-mind-spirit.

All blessings of life come with homework. Unless we learn to embrace the whole package of our life experience we're missing out on the most delightful part—learning the lessons, opening our hearts, growing spiritually.

Filled with love

How small our problems are, how ridiculous, when you look at them from another perspective. Soon after writing the letters above, I looked out the window the entire time while flying to Houston and back home to Washington, DC and realized our problems are small and ridiculous, and that sooner or later they will disappear. I knew I had read that and felt that before, but never as clearly as I did then. Our possibilities are infinite as the land you see from an airplane. You can be in paradise and still carry hell in your mind. Or, you can always see the world from a different perspective, and detach from problems, misery, small options, certain people, and temporary situations. You can detach from everything that makes you a slave to your own weaknesses. I really felt that *now I could let go*. I was the observer of my own life and wrote my first message for the world:

"There is no place to hide on earth. Problems will come with you. The only chance to have peace of mind is to face them, deal with them, and let them go, and trust and build oneself.

"You might believe that you live in perfect harmony with yourself. The truth is that recognizing this is a very important step. It is the beginning of all good things, but it is not enough. If you have your harmony, you are able to have much more: the fulfillment of being able to stand by people, the ability to offer true love, and willingness to make a difference around you. If you have your harmony, you can have the courage to put yourself "at risk" with people, knowing that you only take action in their best interest, loving them truly.
You can also take any undesired reactions they have

---

toward you, knowing that nothing can break you into pieces.

"The nice surprise is that by putting yourself at risk, you can only win because you are being the person who doesn't judge and the one who takes action to help people be fulfilled. You offer yourself infinite possibilities, unlimited keys to an unlimited number of doors. We are on earth to help each other grow. Have the courage to do so.

"Start with people you love from the bottom of your heart, and then see them in everybody else. How would the world be if each of us saw our parents, or our kids, or our loved ones in everybody else?"

Where love is not present, nothing exists—Marin Preda, Romanian novelist

The key is love. It unlocks the door to the best of our abilities, to fulfillment, to happiness, to one's live purpose. Love makes miracles become possible.

I took pictures from the airplane, and associated affirmations with one of them, which I look at daily:

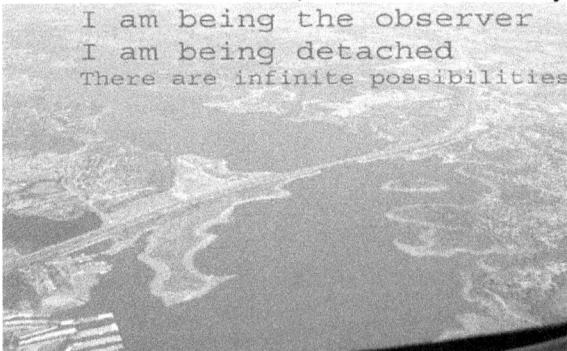

I am being the observer
I am being detached
There are infinite possibilities

74

"Being with people" exercise

Soon after my trip to Houston, a new opportunity to participate in a seminar on personal development appeared. I was more than excited to spend three days with over a hundred people who were all there to transform the way they looked at their lives.

At some point, we formed a big circle together. Each person had someone standing right in front of them, looking into their eyes. After a few minutes, we rotated, so each of us had a chance to "be with" someone else. We looked into each other's eyes, at each other's faces, and explored "being with" each other.

I wasn't afraid of standing and being scanned by their eyes, and I didn't feel uncomfortable, afraid, shy, or embarrassed. Many people were really uncomfortable, though. I wanted so much to give them what they needed and felt so much love for all of them. I perceived their pain, cared about them, and gave them all my positive energy.

Focusing all my energy to mentally give them what they needed most gave me an enormous boost. I felt like levitating.

At some point, my partner was one of my teammates. When I looked into in his eyes, I saw so much purity and peace. It was overwhelming. I smiled and thanked him for being in the world. He was impressed by my tears of joy and told me that he saw humanity in my eyes.

This exercise reminded me of the joy I had doing the exercises my esoteric teacher taught me, and the old times in college when I used to meditate like that with my beloved friend Mirela. Therefore, the "being with people" exercise had a huge impact on my willingness to start my daily meditation again.

At night, I remembered again one of my repeated dreams from childhood. In my grandmother's house was a secret basement, hidden under my favorite room. In the basement was a beautiful treasure—objects made of gold, crystals, and fine fabrics, books and carved mysterious symbols. In the psychology and symbolism of dreams, the hidden room, the basement, represents the unknown, the subconscious mind. My perception was now different. I was now more aware that the room was not a secret. Its existence was not questionable, and even though I didn't know what was inside, it didn't feel strange and untouchable anymore.

Bye-bye, childish thoughts

That weekend I also remembered an event from childhood, and a decision I made when I was three years old. That decision kept coming back to me unconsciously, always when I was facing failure. What happened? I got lost while waiting for my father to get out of a huge grocery line. What I told myself was "I am alone and don't know what to do." This attitude is the opposite of someone's who prays and knows that God is always there for them. When we say "I'm alone," we disregard God and our guardian angels that are always with us.

—

"Life is hard only when we think that we have to figure out everything on our own," I told myself. "Just ask and trust that the will of God will be fulfilled. Don't worry and don't be attached."

Just ask and relax, allowing the answers to be revealed to you.

As I gave up this decision ("I am alone and don't know what to do") I started to perceive the presence of divinity in a totally different way. Being whole, complete, and trusting is the way of being receptive to God, and to the voice of intuition.

The Bridge of Light

I remember who I am

The following week, after an almost ten-year break from my daily meditation, I looked into my own eyes in the mirror and told myself: "It's time!"

Forgiveness and peace of mind, the experience of love versus fear, builds self-esteem and self-love.

I failed the exercise a few times, but had the urge to continue over and over again. I knew that I could do it. I prayed and told myself many empowering things—and it worked. My eyes were pouring tears till they dried, and then I reconnected to my soul, after such a long time. I saw my body made of light again, and had my hands warm again. The voice in my head finally stopped talking—it was quiet. I was able to breathe in peace and felt the power of harmony and love flowing through my veins. It was so wonderful. I had missed it so much.

Then I knew and felt that this was the way to my higher self, to the manifestation of my mission in this world. "I'm not trying to figure things out and be attached to any results anymore. I'm finally back in the process."

I am in harmony with my higher self. I have a solid connection to God's love, through self-love.

That's what was missing before.

———

Then I remembered an old dream in which I was not just able to fly out the window to save myself from evil, but also to carry my friends with me, without falling down to the ground. It was really hard, but I did it. Remembering this dream was a *reminder* of my soul mission, and it came to me to say, "Now, it's possible; keep going."

During meditation, I loved everybody, prayed for everybody, and called on my grandmother, Roza, and my first esoteric teacher to help me and be with me for protection and guidance. I didn't want to disturb them, but I wanted to accomplish my purpose in life, and knew that was worthy of their effort. I told my grandmother, "Help me wipe your tears away, help me bring your daughter back (find a cure for her disease). You gave me the key. I was hearing you while you were talking to people about God. I was your first 'recruit.' I don't want to be alone and enjoy the glory by myself with selfishness." I told my father, "I want to wipe your tears away and be the one who's going to help her. Be on my side! I want you in my life in the greatest way." I wanted to deserve to be allowed to be a tool in God's hands. Ego had to disappear, so my higher self could be alive, awakened, manifesting light and peace.

You experience reality when you are in touch with the best of you.

After that experience, I finally started to act through the mantra "I am connected." I got the power of "community" in my life, at work, in prayers, and in spirituality.

A good practice is to pray every day for yourself and everyone in your spiritual circle.

People from all religions find their deepest connection with the Divine when they pray.

In the life of the Indian there was only one inevitable duty—the duty of prayer—the daily recognition of the Unseen and Eternal.
—Ohiyesa (Charles Eastman), Wahpeton Dakota

That day, for the first time in my life, I had the need to pray for the ones I loved. I wrote everyone's name into a notebook, and prayed for all of them—asking God to help each of them in the way they needed. It was a huge spiritual transformation for me. I was so connected to God, felt such peace of mind, and was also so connected with everyone I prayed for. "Life is so meaningful now!"

We all have light to share

A few days later, someone I didn't even know but who an angel must have sent to me, gave me a very empowering motivational quote that I read every day. It really helped me build more self-confidence and it also inspired me to give more to others. Very soon it became the core of an inspirational session that my dear coworkers and I created with the priceless support of my empowering coach for the students we served.

Our deepest fear is not that we are inadequate. Our deepest fear is that we are powerful beyond measure. It is our light, not our darkness, that most frightens us. We ask ourselves, who am I to be brilliant, gorgeous, talented, and fabulous?

Actually, who are you not to be? You are a child of God. Your playing small doesn't serve the world. There's nothing enlightened about shrinking so that other people won't feel insecure around you. We are all meant to shine, as children do. We are born to make manifest the glory of God that is within us. It's not just in some of us, it's in everyone. And as we let our own light shine, we unconsciously give other people permission to do the same. As we are liberated from our own fear, our presence automatically liberates others.
—Marianne Williamson

What a blessing to have a boss who knows that people are a mirror of one's relationship to God, though love, someone who knows that love is not about what you get but about what you are able to give. By supporting me to put together the inspirational session, she gave me the opportunity to *give*, and get a glimpse of how wonderful it is to be on a spiritual mission.

Through these sessions, hundreds of people were inspired to give back to their communities in many ways. Many found the joy of giving in their heart besides just having more self-confidence and self-determination. For three months, while working on that project, I practiced being a support for people's greatness, while never working alone.

To my delight, two of my dearest friends were creating and developing the project into something bigger than I thought it could ever be. They didn't limit the project to an inspirational session for the participants, but challenged the participants' imagination and stimulated them to reach out and help their communities.

Some were implementing educational programs for women, others were mentoring, others were feeding the homeless, and so on.

Teamwork became a habit, an expectation from life. It opened up a new realm of possibilities for me, who used to think that "I am on my own."

The distance between having skills and being the skills (becoming) is diminished by practicing and being willing to face everything that stands in our way. This is the difference between observing life and living life.

Thank you, dear team of wonderful friends. Thank you, coaches. Thank you, givers and receivers. We were all filling our hearts with joy and love.

Nurturing my roots

As soon as the project was accomplished, I went back to Romania to visit my parents and friends. What a wonderful time we had together.

During the second day, my friends and I went to visit the village museum. It was such a delightful experience to reconnect with Romanian tradition and values. It filled my heart with joy and fulfillment.
Since I spent so much of my childhood in the countryside, the village museum helped me feel like a child again. It helped me become grounded—feel my roots going deep into the ground, sustaining the tree of life within. What immigrant doesn't feel the need to recharge with the vibration of their homeland?

Traditional Romanian painted eggs

While at my parents' house, I was listening to their stories and spending wonderful days with them, looking at old photos of the entire family. My heart expanded seeing how loved I've always been by my family. Love was felt and acknowledged in a new, profound way—like never before. I was just letting it all in, and felt that the power of love and connection with my dear family is the source of my power within.

I have asked God that my grandmother be my spiritual guide, and I perceived that she is with me and that she'll help me to sustain my mom. I always thought that it would be too hard for me to protect my mom because she would overwhelm and drain me, but when I accepted her illness, and accepted to help her, a huge boundary between us vanished.

I gave her a picture of my eyes, as they looked after twenty minutes of meditation thinking of her, and told her to look at that picture any time she needs my help and support.

That was a huge step for me, to make myself so vulnerable to her needs and to give her bio-energy through my eyes without notice. However, my faith in my grandmother's help made me look at myself as being the earthly connection between her and the unseen forces of the universe that would actually support her. That is the essence of channeling. I finally got that I don't have to even try to help her by myself, but just to be a wheel in a sophisticated mechanism that I don't even need to understand. A lot of pressure vanished and way more joy and faith replaced it.

Recognizing a soul-family member

My cousin Tiberiu and I have known each other for lifetimes. When I was in elementary school, and he was a little boy, I remember a moment when, visiting his family, all of a sudden we both looked at each other and connected deeply, and in my heart, I said, "I missed you so much." At that time, I had no clue about the idea of reincarnation. My statement didn't make any sense to me, so I dismissed it right away. That was my first experience of recognizing a soul-family member.

We were now happy to see each other again. He told me that my values will change, and things that now matter to me will not matter anymore soon.
I was a little scared and resistant to the idea, but later, as that happened, it was so natural. He also reminded me that God loves me, and that any hardship coming my way will be meant to make me stronger. Later on, I had my cousin's words in mind every time I was tested by God, and that gave me a huge amount of confidence. We meditated together and had visions about each other.

———

Peaceful choices

I had so much love back home. When I returned to the U.S., after my trip to Romania, I was ready to start a spiritual marathon. My dear friend Geny pointed this out before my departure. "You are now ready to go through anything life throws at you. You are filled with love." It was true and I very much needed to hear it, especially since at that point I was just starting a new social life as well.

My life partner and I were now on different pathways, after twelve years of being together. We were at total peace with our decision, but habits are powerful, attachments are strong, identity changes, and emotions are stirred up—all at once—in such moments of transition. We were fortunate to have had learned to look into the eyes of *truth* and see what it is and what it is not, and give up any resentments toward each other and toward ourselves.

In no time, we got to relate with each other as *true friends*, and our *true* friendship became whole and complete *because* we divorced. This was our karmic reason to meet in this life—to repair our thousands-year-old friendship that was broken in the previous life in which we met. We were not true to each other while denying our unhappiness as a couple, but now we were.

We also realized that he was supposed to learn something about spirituality from me, and I was supposed to learn something about family from him. The learning takes place by our own life's example. We are very fortunate to be so clear about this *life purpose*, *karma*, and *lessons to learn*. And I see how without this knowledge we might have failed it all together again.

Cords of bliss

A few days after my return to the United States, while browsing through the photos taken in Romania, I had a vision about my mom. It was so intense, it almost took me out of consciousness. There was so much love, and it was so deep, it took my breath away. I tried to put on paper what I felt, in Romanian, but still words are not enough…

To my mother:
Your green eyes are the infinite green fields of hope
Your pure thoughts are the colorful wild flowers
Your shining face, your beautiful smile, your wisdom,
your courage, your vulnerability
Are breaking through eons and reaching out to my soul;

Your spirit becomes Divine Love
You are the symbol of Feminine Grace and Power
I wonder, "when did we meet first?"

You called me through times, to come back to you,
through you,

To help me awaken in spirit,
To teach me about love and compassion, about giving,
about receiving....

You, just by being you, are helping me transform in the
flowing fountain of life, giving water.
You are my source; you are the key opening the magic
doors toward my power within.
I love you in a Divine way, and feel you over lifetimes

Your purity takes my breath away
You are the Feminine Power, the Goddess
And I'm now discovering the feminine powers in me like
never before
Through my love for you

My cord of light is piercing through infinite space toward
you
And I know that this is our divine moment of connecting
in spirit
And I am reborn through my love for you, to a new life,
given to God.

I am reborn through my love for you, to a new life, given
to God.

Reborn in Spirit

Focused on light

By focusing on what's really important to you, you allow others to do the same.
— Esther and Jerry Hicks (the Teachings of Abraham)

The next day, I woke up, and started in a totally different way than ever before—with sixty minutes of bliss, which consisted of: praying and thanking God for all the blessings in my life; reading my list of goals and my vision of my life; and then meditating. When I meditated, I practiced the meditations given by my esoteric teacher, and also affirmations—this time only for fifteen minutes a day, as he had taught me. At the end, I lay down and practiced breathing exercises and deep relaxation for another fifteen minutes.

Many books and people inspired me to create this empowering recipe, which I am sharing with you at the end of this volume. Even though I had it in mind for a while before starting to practice, only after my spiritual rebirth through love could I find the power within and the self-determination to put all pieces of the puzzle together and to do it every day.

These were the most inspiring sources for me to create this *Ninety-Day Empowerment Recipe*:
* My teacher's gifts
* Inspiring people in my life
* The Holy Bible
* *The Psychology of Achievement* by Brian Tracy

---

* *Thoughts Are Things* by Prentice Mulford
* *How to Get What You Really, Really, Really, Really Want* by Dr. Wayne Dyer and Deepak Chopra
* *Ask and It Is Given* by Esther and Jerry Hicks (the Teachings of Abraham)

First, I prayed and made a pact with my teacher's soul: "Please be with me, guide me, and protect me. I promise to be patient and practice your teachings steadily, and look for long-term results rather than random miracles." That was the moment when I felt inspired to start writing *this book*. By doing so, and writing about him, our connection became more and more powerful.

I also prayed for his soul every morning. I found a photo of a white horse flying through white and purple clouds and pasted it on my collage of pictures. It was clear to me that the white horse in my early dream—"the Colorful Stars"—was the representation of my esoteric teacher, who I met soon after that life-transforming dream. Later on, I often referred to him as being the "white horse" in my conversation with my spiritual partners and friends.

My house became a sacred and peaceful place, connecting me with my greatness. By setting up the background—the context—of my life, I was able to build a beautiful life experience.

Just a few days after I started this empowering ritual, people told me that there was something very different about me. They felt my whole aura changing. My palms started to tingle very often.

***

A few weeks later, my dear friend Geny sent me a present in the mail from Romania: a book written by Prentice Mulford, *Thoughts Are Things,* which my esoteric teacher had translated from English to Romanian many years ago. It made me cry with joy and much love for her. She was the messenger for the tremendous support I needed— to have a tangible, written reminder from my teacher. Reading the book, I felt a huge force within me and a very strong connection with my teacher. In the foreword, he described the way Prentice Mulford died—by choosing not to come back from his astral trip during meditation, and cutting his silver cord. I was amazed and wondered, "Did you do the same thing at the end of your life?" and the answer came "Yes." That was different from a prayer or a request: it was my first direct question for my teacher's spirit.

Ever since, he stopped being *the memory of* my esoteric teacher. He revived for me, and he became part of my life, just like my family and friends were. From the spirit world, he came little by little. I started to feel his presence clearly during meditation. He has always been with me in my spiritual practices, and later, while teaching reiki.

Sometimes he came in my mind during prayers as a huge globe of light. I would say, "God, please give light to my teacher's soul," and immediately I visualized lightning bolts filling a big globe of light. Later on, I was told by a medium that he's now associated with other powerful spirits and that's the way he makes himself seen. Those were clairvoyant experiences, but at the time I didn't know what they were. I thought it was just my imagination.

Globe of light

***

Here is one of the great lessons I got out of *Thoughts Are Things*: when you can't focus on one thing, you rush. When you rush, you become afraid. When you rush, you are not present to your initial thought and spoil its value and the pleasure of having it. If you can focus on one thing, you can ignore pain. You can save yourself from evil by keeping your thoughts on its opposite. I grasped why it is so important to master your mind as you open the unseen doors: to protect yourself. It is amazing. That's why my teacher told me to work on my ability to think about one thing at a time, as I started to open the unseen doors of the spirit world.

That night I got some related "practical training" during sleep. It seemed as if I was in my room, but some force was keeping me stuck in one place, I was not able to walk. I lit a candle that was nearby, but the force blew it out and there I was in the dark again. I tried to reach out to my wooden holy cross on the shelf, but the unseen force took it away. That seemed pretty serious to me. Fear tried to take over for a moment, but then I heard, deep in my heart:

92

Focus on light!

And so light was filling my chest—the candle was within. I kept focusing on light, and ignored the fear, ignored the feeling of being vulnerable due to not being able to walk. Soon, the candle within took the shape of a cross of light … so I discovered that:

True light and faith are inside of me.

My joy was huge. The peace became so profound. I was released from the trap and woke up safely. This was a dream of extreme clarity and it seemed very real.

Beside the importance of focusing on light, another very important thing occurred to me that night, which later I've shared with all of my students.

Our number one guardian angel is our pure heart. Vanity is a trap even for many people who dedicate their whole life to spirituality. Dark beings wish to give us spiritual gifts, and then use us. We have to find the power within to give up the possibility of receiving any spiritual gifts, rather than selling our souls. We need to work on our self-healing for as long as is needed to become pure hearted, and only then ask for spiritual gifts. Being pure hearted doesn't mean being perfect, for the purpose of life is to always grow and learn.

Your guardian angel is your pure heart.

Reading *The Power of Awareness* by Neville Goddard gave me a reinforcement of the importance of focusing on what I want.

———

It also encouraged me to dream more, and actually get back into the habit of dreaming about already being who I want to be, and having what I want to have.

True love is based on one's faith in God. When we depend on something outside of ourselves it's because we're disconnected from our light within. Therefore, the way out from the frustration and suffering of not having what we want is the reconnection with our light within through prayer, meditation, and powerful intent.

***

My mom sent me a beautiful poem, written long ago by the elders of our nation. Along the way was the most powerful reinforcement of my attitude of gratitude.

Blessing for the home:

Where there is faith
There is love

Where there is love
There is peace

Where there is peace
There is blessing

Where there is blessing
There is God

Where there is God
There is no need.

Every time I was in any kind of need, after reading this, I knew that I was disconnected from God, and that every moment of resistance, sadness, complaint, dissatisfaction, or worry does no good and, even worse, attracts bad energy, bad guidance, and doesn't serve me in any way. I shifted my day by choice. I wrote down what I was grateful for and everything changed.

***

While reading *The Power of Now* by Eckhart Tolle, I realized that being present means putting the book aside and continue talking with the wonderful person who started a very meaningful conversation. Without the willingness to apply what we read and what we're taught, we can't move forward too much. Information is not enough—it only feeds the mind. Action, though, models and feeds the spirit. We exchanged many inspirational thoughts and one of them that made me feel more tuned in to the Life Force Energy was this:

God is Truth and God is Love
God is Love and that's the Truth

***

It was almost Christmas time. As usual in the morning, I was watching my "people collage" (the photographs of my dear family and friends), praying for each and every one. As on every morning, when I got to pray for my friend Virgil, who had passed over right after college, I wanted to say: "God, please send light to his spirit, and take away the sorrow of his parents," but somehow, I said "my parents" instead.

—

I realized that it was him talking through me. It felt so real, and made me cry tears of joy. I called his parents right away and shared the story with them. They told me how much they miss him at that time of the year, and how much they wanted a sign from him. My sharing gave them joy and as I said goodbye it felt as if Virgil was there, thanking me for delivering the message.

That day it became clear to me that:

The higher self is a spark of God, is our connection with God. As we reveal our light more and more, are more and more one *with our higher self, many powers within are activated. These powers are not the goal, they are the effect of being connected with the higher self: intuition, peace of mind, wisdom, balance, focus, real presence, spiritual connections, healing abilities, and clairvoyance. Universal Consciousness is the key to infinite possibilities.*

Soon after that, while still practicing every morning my empowerment recipe, I saw the movie *The Secret*. It was amazing to me how much my recipe was tuned in to the same thing—the Law of Attraction.
At the same time, though, I realized that it made perfect sense to get such confirmations from different sources since there is just one Truth, and everyone tuning in to Universal Consciousness receives it. The shape is different, but the essence is the same.

Carmen, one of the six people I've watched the movie with, pointed out: "Speak aloud with God! Read from the Bible every day and ask God questions. Be focused on one thing. We are trying to reach God in so many different ways instead of going straight to Him."

It was my first time meeting Carmen. However, it felt as if we had known one another for eons. Her powerful energy had the same source as mine: daily meditation.

It is said that when you start following your soul mission, you meet more and more of your soul-family members. Carmen is definitely one of my dear soul-family members, and our friendship and spiritual partnership has developed more and more along the years.

***

Someone asked me if I'm always happy. My answer was: "Only a liar or an insane person could pretend that. I'm not always happy, but I've learned how to drag myself out of a bad mood way faster than before." In fact, I have had moments of sadness and depression along the way— as long as I resisted my own transformation. Sometimes meditation seemed so painful, I had to force myself to do it. Later on, after the ninety days, sometimes I skipped it, and as a result, my day felt without substance.
As a water sign, my emotions were also running the show sometimes. I noticed how, in melancholic moments, my first impulse was to not talk with anyone, go home, and stay in bed, over thinking. However, now being aware that "thoughts are things," the responsibility of my own creation forced me to give up emotional moments much more quickly.

***

Around that time, one of my friends who I cared about and to whom I was very attracted got the flu. I touched his neck with my palms for a minute, wishing that he would feel better, but at the same time, I was disturbed by my attraction for him. I gave up trying to give him energy for the moment, and took my hands off him. At night, after a very powerful meditation session, I touched his neck again in my thoughts, and focused only on his health. I kept my eyes closed the entire time and focused on him being healthy, laughing, and I visualized my hands on him the entire time. My hands were so warm it was painful, and I noticed the power of my thoughts and my care for him. The next day, I made a joke and told him that I did "witcheries" on him at night, and he said that at that exact time he woke up and was sweating, then he felt much better.

That was my first experience of practicing distant healing, without being taught. Perhaps old skills from past lives awaken through the desire to see dear ones being well.

***

These were highlights from my life during the ninety days of practicing my empowerment recipe. It was quite a journey, and a huge positive shift in me was seen by everyone in my life. After the ninety days, I stopped reading my goals daily, and I replaced reading my gratefulness list with writing what I most love in my beloved family and friends. I continued with my meditations, and changed the affirmations.

A person's main task in life is to give birth to oneself.
—Erich Fromm, psychoanalyst and philosopher

—

The last barrier is broken

By writing down and sharing my empowerment recipe, my passion for coaching and teaching was triggered. I took up being a coach for a "self-expression" program. I was so committed to my participants and the accomplishment of their dreams. I also had the feeling that I would learn something very important.

It was a three-month rollercoaster, but really worth it. The commitment and love I had for my participants allowed me to find strength, power, inspiration, and radiant energy, even when otherwise I would have been melancholic, turned inward, and unwilling to be in action. No matter how my day went, when a coaching call came I would shift every time to a grounded, peaceful, and powerful state of mind. However, soon I realized that at the end of the call, I was drained of energy, tired, and filled with everybody's issues. Moreover, anxiety crippled me, and I had a fear of failure. I was seeing how I was getting enrolled in my participants' problems, rather than being the observer and the catalyst.

It seemed that love was not enough. My friend Carmen advised me to detach and not take on people's problems, and to just let the energy flow. She told me that I have to learn how to protect myself if I want to be a healer. It was very true and valuable advice, but how could I do that? Well, the truth is within and it had already been presented to me many times in my dreams, through life lessons, through friends, and through books. All I had to do was to face it and decide to do something about it.

As I was learning to be a coach, I had a coach to guide me. He helped me sort it all out. He asked me:

"Are you your feelings or do you have feelings?"
"I am my feelings."
"Who are you without your feelings?"
"I don't know."

Resistance slipped in, but since now it was obvious to me that without dealing with this I couldn't be a healer, I was willing to cooperate.

"What are you telling yourself?" he asked.
"Life would be total nonsense and I would feel like I'm dead without my feelings. This is how I have lived my life so far," I said, still feeling like that was the truth, but then I realized that being attached comes from being identified with my feelings.

This was why I was looking for strong feelings, and unconsciously I looked forward for any kind of strong feelings (not only joy and pleasure, but also sadness, strong desire, pain, depression, everything that everyone else feels, everything that I would feel if I were in the other's skin).

While talking, I realized the importance of listening to my own conversations in the moment.

"Are you willing to give this up?" he asked.

The whole earth vanished under my feet. It was so hard, so painful, almost impossible. In fact, if it hadn't been for my faith, that which is a must for me to be a healer, I would have clearly said "no."
After a few moments of silence though, with tears in my eyes, I said:

"Yes, I'm giving up being identified with my feelings."
"Good. What's now present for you?" he asked.

A few more moments of silence followed. With amazement, I said:

"Void ... Peace ... Clarity ... Power ... Love ... Harmony.... It's a miracle!"

Unbelievable! I was so much more than my feelings. We all are, but some of us just don't know.

The subsequent coaching calls with my group were so much more productive. Being detached, I was able to be present and truly listen. It didn't mean that I didn't care—not at all. Better results in my participants' lives were a great measurement of my care and love for them.

To make an analogy, imagine your best friend is in a lake and does not know how to swim. She is likely to drown. What would you do? Would you be emotional while trying to drag her out or would you stay calm, focused, and pull her out, by her hair if necessary, to save her life?

I have feelings, but I'm not my feelings. Taking myself out of the way, I can be just an antenna, a channel of energy from the universe into others. Having no need to feed my feelings and emotions creates no desire to blend with others' energy, good or bad, and instead gives me more power to be of service for the highest good.

***

That was my most important lesson learned from serving as a coach. As soon as I really accepted, practiced, and learned it, I was unexpectedly exposed to vital information about how to become a healer, and about what's available for healers nowadays in the United States. The source of this information was a CD called *Chakra Healing* by Rosalyn Bruyere.

Listening to that CD, my calling became extremely powerful.

"Here and now it's all real! I don't have to find a guru or have healing in my life just for myself and my circle of friends, as it was back in Romania during Communism.

I can go to school, and one day I'll be a professional healer and teacher."

The possibility of it created a very powerful feeling of urgency.

"I am unstoppable, fully self-expressed, free and powerful beyond measure, and I choose to be true to myself and my deepest desire."

A few days later I declared in front of a room full of people:

Who I am is the possibility of being a healer of body, mind, and spirit!

Back to my childhood bliss

Something amazing happened: ten days later I started to learn about being a healer of body-mind-spirit, by starting classes at a massage school. Nothing seemed to be a barrier for me. For the first time in my life, I was happy to be broke, having no idea how I was going to pay for school, but I trusted God that the universe would find a way, and I accepted doing whatever it took to make it happen.

Going to massage school gave me even more fulfillment that I had imagined. Learning anatomy, physiology, and pathology helped me build the body-mind-spirit bridge. I was fascinated with the miracle that we all are, without even being aware of it.
I also met so many wonderful people and found so much information about healing arts. Additionally, I got back to the basics of my childhood—massage.

To me, massage is the manifestation of genuine love and care. I grew up receiving from my grandmother, Mama Nana, and giving to my father on a regular basis, and I continued to do so later in college, with my roommates and best friends. As soon as school started, I wondered how in the world I had lived without it for a good number of years.

Besides, every time I was giving a massage, I would set my intent toward healing, breathing in light through the top of my head and breathing out light through my hands and into my classmates who were receiving the massage. It was divine.

One of my instructors said he saw my energy rising up to the ceiling, while I massaged a classmate and was praying to God to allow me to be a healing tool.

A glimpse of Oneness

My daily meditation and prayer became the root of my life, and even a habit. It didn't require a great deal of effort anymore to keep it consistent. Sometimes, during the weekends, when I was able to ignore the clock, my meditation went up to three hours. My whole body changed. It felt almost like the flight of a feather in the wind. My hands were tingling more and more often. My thoughts and emotions were more joyful, my whole being, more radiant.

One of the insights I got during meditation was this: praying for the soul of my esoteric teacher, I asked God to give him light. I then saw thunderbolts going straight to his soul, which was represented by a huge globe of light.

Then, somehow, I was inside the globe for a second, and it occurred to me that I had access to all his spiritual gifts and to all his power. I could be given all magic gifts at the snap of a finger. *Wow!*

That day and very often afterwards, I felt so blessed just for having the chance to meet him, and for everything else … for my grandparents, parents, friends, and relatives who touched my soul and gave me the chance to learn so much from them and manifest my love. It was a matter of faith and the capacity to allow it to happen. I was at peace, calm and powerful, most of the time.

I can claim any spiritual gifts. The miracle is already inside of me, and so it is in everyone.

***

An essential change occurred with regard to my motivation: in my childhood, the main conscious reason for my desire to be a healer was my mom's condition. Later on, healing myself from emotional traumas, a shift occurred: my calling to be a healer wasn't based on suffering, lack of acceptance, or fear anymore, but rather on a sense of life purpose, possibility, love, inspiration, and power.

The most inspiring message for me is the one Jesus gave to the Samaritan woman:

Whosoever drinketh of this water shall thirst again: But whosoever drinketh of the water that I shall give him shall never thirst; but the water that I shall give him shall be in him a well of water springing up into everlasting life.
—John 4:13–14

In my words: "If you drink this water, you'll be thirsty again, but if you drink the water I'm offering you, not only will you never be thirsty again, but you'll transform in a flowing fountain of life-giving water."

This message inspired me to *become* and *be* that fountain. Based on that, I created a more powerful affirmation, with a mystical connotation:

I am a river of love

I am a flowing fountain of life-giving water

I am a light in other people's lives

Looking in the mirror into my own eyes and saying that aloud was the most empowering experience to me. It was almost like invoking a higher spirit that would come down into me. My hands were warm and filled with white-golden light, my eyes piercing, my breathing slow, and my spirit wide awake. I am *one* with my higher self. As we grow in spirit, we can spread the light around us. Every single good vibe matters.

As a direct result of daily meditation, I was alert. That helped me see with ease any lesson that had to be learned. Inspiration started to flow more and more. Connections between the physical world and the mystical interpretation of life were now made clear to me every day.

***

I read from the book *Ask and It Is Given* by Esther and Jerry Hicks (the Teachings of Abraham) about how to talk to yourself when you're sick: "Each cell of my body is a natural healer, and knows how to heal even if I don't." And then, having learned in my anatomy book that the human body is made out of 75–100 trillion healers, I told myself:

I am made of 100 trillion healers.

The thought gave me power, and confidence not only for me, but for everyone else's healing. We are a miracle. And we all share these miracles. How much do we *not* have in common? That is totally insignificant. We are all branches of the same tree of life.

A few days later during meditation, my mom came to my mind, and associated with her, a certainty: *You will be healed in this life.* Then her mom, my dear grandmother Roza, came in my mind, smiling.

Because I am human

Life was good. However, a lesson I've learned is that transformation takes time, and the high vibrations have to be maintained. And, not even then is happiness one hundred percent guaranteed. Even with all my meditations, affirmations, massages, big dreams, wonderful friends, and tremendous family, I still experienced moments of depression and sadness. The theme of those moments was my romantic life.

"I'm lost and I don't know what to do," my old false identity was saying.

Due to my awareness of the power of thought, it took me less and less time at this point to shift.

"What are you looking for? The love is 'home,' inside of you. It's your love for *all that is*," my soul knew.

When we are connected to the light inside of us, there is no place for being lost and confused.

So I just kept empowering myself with positive affirmations:

"Who I am is the possibility of being a healer of body, mind, and spirit. I'm giving up feeling lost, on my own, and confused. I am the source of my life. I'm cause in the matter and I am responsible for my happiness today, as well as my happiness and fulfillment in the future."

Constant empowering self-talk is a great tool for pulling ourselves back up. Yes, we can! It's our choice! Life is beautiful!

Destiny embraced

A good friend introduced me to Bob Hickman, one of the most famous mediums in the area. I was fascinated with the idea of meeting a *true* psychic, so I booked an hour. The first thing he told me was: "You are a channel of energy. You have all spiritual gifts, you just have to remember."

It felt really good to hear that. I needed a confirmation of my ongoing transformation, and he told me even more— about the possibility of becoming just like him, just like my teacher, just as I had wanted all my life.

"You have four spiritual guides, bringing you energy from the four directions.

"In your last past life, you were a gypsy healer, and you were killed by the Nazis in the 1940s. You were very upset about the atrocities you had seen, and your last words were:
>*I will return and I will heal the world.*

"Then, you chose to be born in Communism, to face the possibility of failing your purpose. You chose all those barriers and obstacles just to straighten your self-determination."

As soon as I heard about being killed by the Nazis, one of my dreams in which I was killed came to mind…. The dream was half filled with symbols, and now it made perfect sense.

"Learn how to protect yourself. Detach even more. You've come a long way."

"Am I going to become a clairvoyant?" I asked.

"You already are, you just have to find your way. You'll see through the walls, and do remote viewing. Continue with your daily meditation. Look into a lit candle. You'll get there."

"Am I going to be a true healer?"

"Yes, *it is your destiny*. You've done healing already, but not consistently. You were a true healer in many past lives and you know very well what you're doing, even though you're not aware of it. In less than a year you'll have all the healing tools you need."

"Can you tell me anything about Mr. Alexandru E. Russu?" (All I told Bob was his name.)

"Yes. He's coming to you at night and leads your spirit during your astral traveling, and during your meditations. He was very powerful during his lifetime and now he's even more powerful. He's now associated with other powerful spirits in a globe of light"

"Wow, he comes to my mind like this while praying for him," I noticed.

"Bob, does my teacher have any message for me?" I asked, while my heart was beating with huge excitement.

"Yes, he says that he wants to talk to his little one." (In Romanian, *little one* is translated *fetita mea*, as he used to call me.)

"You have learned well, my daughter. I was with you as you have been writing your book and I will continue to be with you. If I had many students, there were few that understood deeply, as you did. You have captured, in essence, all my teachings. You have written in a way that will allow many generations to come, and to see, and to know, and to hear the very experience that I thought to teach you, and now they will learn from you.

"You have heard my voice many times.

"Your writing is giving me life on earth again.

"The books will come, yes, and there will be more, but my words, if they don't stay in your heart, have no value to anyone.

"It is in your heart *where I want your teachings to begin and to stay."*

Wow! I needed a few moments of complete silence after this incredible message, coming through the medium Bob, from my esoteric teacher.

I could still feel his presence, just like I'd been feeling it during meditation. It was overwhelming me with pure love and joy. I missed him so much and tears were falling down my face. But at the same time, his message had just given me the ultimate evidence of our eternal connection. Why would I miss him when he had always been with me?

"You were pregnant and had an abortion a long time ago," Bob continued. "You don't carry any sin for that. It was an agreement between you and the soul of the child, from the spirit world, that you'll be taught a lesson about humanity. The experience awakened in you maternal feelings that are necessary on your spiritual journey. The child's spirit did not suffer, it happened just the way it was supposed to."

Wow, what a huge relief!

Bob gave me so much spiritual joy and confidence. I went home and sat on a chair looking in vain and thinking over all he said, and realized that:

My entire journey led me not toward "reinventing" myself as a healer of body, mind, and spirit, but toward remembering my destiny.

Then, all of the sudden my eyes were caught by the poster I'd had by my bed for over a year: an American Indian poster representing four diverse spiritual guides gathering energy from the four directions.

"*Wow*, this poster is the representation of my spiritual guides! This is why I was so attracted by it."

That night I looked at my poster for a long time, meditated on it, and connected to what Bob said it represented—my guides.

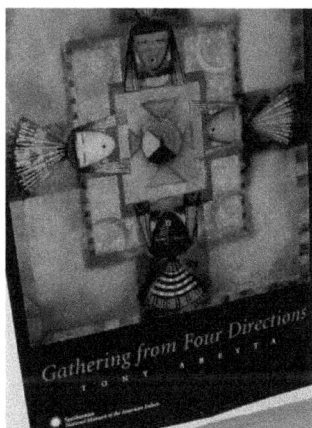

Gathering from four directions

The whole world was mine. "Yes, it is true, this is my destiny." Lots of ideas about how to serve as a healer popped into my mind. I spent half a day dreaming like a child about how I was going to manifest it all, and wrote everything down on paper.

It took me 33 years of my life to really awaken and take full charge of my spiritual mission.

God, we really need a lot of patience!

When you follow your heart
You are on your chart
Easy or hard
The lesson is taught
And the mission is found

It is time!

A few days later, I had an insight during meditation: "Don't tell anyone (about your dreams) for six weeks. Preserve your power to blossom more quickly." In the next few days, I tried to not talk about my dreams, but when in a conversation with one of my friends, it seemed to me that my sharing would help her overcome a big barrier, I did. "I give up my quick blossoming for that. It is worthy. I would rather blossom a little bit later and be here for others in the moment."

***

One of my best friends had been in a very difficult situation that had constantly gotten worse to the point where he felt like life was too miserable to deal with. He wasn't answering the phone, which wasn't a good sign to me. My first reaction was to despair and cry, but then I remembered that being emotional doesn't help. Instead, I thought a sharp spirit and the right action taken at the right time might help.

True soul love is the key to healing, the foundation of any powerful prayer. Burning sage, lighting candles, and praying for him from all my heart, I hoped that he'd call me back, but he didn't. It was hard to be calm, knowing his situation, and knowing that his grandpa had committed suicide. For some reason, the story of his grandpa popped into my mind as soon as he didn't answer the phone.

With my holy cross and the Holy Bible on his photo, I kneeled and begged God to unbound him from any possible curse or karmic pattern related to his grandpa's death. I asked my guides to leave me to help him, and pour light on him, and rejuvenate his soul.

Praying to Jesus, my connection with Divinity jumped to a higher level, to a place of peace, a place of knowing that all was well…. And right then, he finally called me back. He admitted that he had had self-destructive thoughts but then all of a sudden he felt relieved and saw life from a different perspective. I can't describe my joy and gratefulness to God.

***

My cousin Tania was diagnosed with an aneurysm, and had to have brain surgery. All our family decided to pray for her together, right before the surgery. Seven of us prayed for her—six were in Romania, while I was in Washington, DC, just sixty miles away from her.

We all started at the same time, without communicating about any particular sequence to our prayer. So I started by praying for her, then for the doctors, then for us—the seven people praying for her—only to find later that two other cousins from Romania were doing the exact same thing, at the exact same time.

After fifteen minutes, I felt a tremendous amount of power, as if we were all *one*. I prayed and asked that my own spirit guides leave me and take care of her, until she was safe. And indeed, that day I felt extremely vulnerable.

When I left my house that day, I left her photo on my desk, with the holy cross and lit candles on it. I was certain that the distance didn't matter, that wherever someone is in the world, prayers, good intentions, and thoughts being sent right to them will reach them. I visualized Tania surrounded by a white-golden light that was flowing through her whole body. She was safe, healthy, calm, protected, and much loved.

About an hour after our prayer ended, Tania, Dan, her husband, and their daughter, who were all waiting in the hospital's corridors, all of the sudden started to laugh, tell jokes, and feel relaxed as if there were waiting to go into the theater, not a surgery room. Dan told me later that he couldn't recall how many years had passed since he'd felt so much peace in his heart.

The surgery was successful. It was very hard and traumatizing, but life-saving. Two days later, I went to see her. She couldn't open her mouth or her eyes, and couldn't walk or talk. She was in great pain, but conscious and strong. My cousins from Romania were already reiki masters at the time, and practiced distance healing. We spoke and set up a distant healing session while I was in the hospital. My cousin Vali, who is like a soul-sister to me, said that she'd work through me.

So, I placed my hands on Tania and prayed for a full hour, calling on God, on Jesus, on Tania's spiritual guides, and on my spiritual guides and healer guides. Breathing in light through the top of my head, and breathing out light into her hands, I was praying that all the healing light my cousins from Romania were sending would flow into her as she needed, only as much as she could take, for her highest good.

I felt that I was receiving more that she needed and blocked the flow accordingly. How? I have no idea. I wasn't taught how, but knew, just like Bob said I would. Spiritual guidance is always there for us, when we ask for it.

We don't need to know everything, but we need to have faith, and let love lead our way.

At some point, my hands were hurting a lot, and I felt that she was sucking the energy out like a vacuum. After the session, Tania was sleepy so I left for lunch with her husband. My throat, my hands, my heart, and the top of my head felt like vortexes of energy. It was a very distinct sensation. I was dizzy and felt very tired.

Two hours later, we came back and couldn't believe what we saw. Tania was awake, and she was able to open her swollen eye. She also opened her mouth and spoke with us, and even ate a little bit. Her pain was no longer so unbearable, and with our help, she got up and walked a longer distance than even she expected. We were all very happy about the positive impact the prayer and group healing session had had on her. The doctor sent her home a day early, and said that she'd recovered faster than usual.

This event was the last activator for me to start taking a reiki class and become a certified healing arts practitioner. A few days later, a great opportunity appeared out of the blue and I signed up for it.

***

Two weeks before the class started, I had a trip in Los Angeles. I love Southern California very much, but all my plans of enjoying the area were ruined by the flu. I was so sick. I almost couldn't talk or walk. I had a high fever, dizziness, and a sore throat. It was so hard to find any amount of will power to pray, but it seemed that my guides wanted me to see that I could help myself more than I thought. Keeping my hands on my chest and my throat for about an hour, I felt a lot of tingling and heat coming out. There was also joy, peace, and comfort, as a baby feels when a mother nurtures him or her. I was nurtured by my guides, and it felt so good. My flu melted enough for me to enjoy the next day.

***

The following Sunday afternoon there was a reiki fair in Alexandria Old Town. I was still taking classes at the massage school, and I was tired after a long week at work and a long weekend at school. I really wanted to go, but my body wanted to go home and rest. My guides, though, knew that getting a reiki session right before I was supposed to start taking a reiki class was very important.

So I planned on driving home, but missed the exit. I didn't know where I was going, I wanted to turn around, but I got lost again. I kept going. I wanted to take a left but one-way streets didn't let me do it, so I took a right.

By now, it was clear to me that I was not lost but led by my spiritual guides toward the reiki fair. I was supposed to experience the reiki session. I didn't argue with my intuition and got there just in time, despite the usual chaos of the area. Indeed, the reiki session gave me a great taste of how it is to receive, and also, how one is able to serve by becoming a reiki practitioner.

Obviously, the increasing number of opportunities to serve as a healer was telling me that I was ready for the next chapter of my life: becoming a reiki master and teacher. This chapter of my life and more is shared in my book *Reiki and the Path to Enlightenment.*

Our spiritual journey leads us not toward "reinventing" ourselves, but rather toward remembering who we really are, and accomplishing our soul mission. When we finally understand, accept, and start following our soul mission, we find bliss in our hearts.

Tools for Spiritual Development and Spiritual Healing

A Ninety-Day Empowerment Recipe

Below is my empowerment recipe in more detail. I wrote it at the end of the ninety days of daily practice. It had a great impact on me and I encourage you to try it.

The context of our life creates the content of our life. Create a powerful context in ninety days.

Self-discipline is the foundation for achieving all hopes and dreams.
—Rod Terry, the author of *Hope Chest—A Treasure of Spiritual Keepsakes*

A: Ninety days of self-empowerment and discipline will shift your entire life to a higher level

Gratefulness: Start a gratefulness journal. Put on paper all the things that you are most grateful for in life. If you write for ten minutes every morning, it might take you a few weeks. Then, continue by writing down everything that you love in each person in your life, and everything you thank them for. Remember every little thing. When I did that, I also placed a photo of each dear one in my journal.

I started with my grandmothers, my parents, and then continued till my entire notebook was filled. It is so overwhelming and so connecting, I couldn't thank more than one person a day.

When you feel as if you have finished writing, read from your gratefulness journal every morning. It will keep your heart vibrating with joy, it will help you overcome disappointment, and it will attract more things that you'll be grateful for in life. Just be in harmony with this vibration. It's a *habit* to be happy—or to be sad. Create the habit of being grateful by counting your blessings every day. That's the key for a happy life.

I included in my list:

I am grateful because I was born into a family that motivated me to be spiritual
I am grateful that I met so and so … (I list each name)
I am grateful that I am in good health
I am grateful for my experiences of living in love
I am grateful for understanding that the greatest power in the universe is the power of love
I am grateful for living in the U.S.
I am grateful for my connection with nature and animals during childhood.

Goals: Put your goals on paper. Think about "what," not about "how." "How" would limit your dreams. Dream like a child. Keep in mind that everything that you can think about, and are excited about, you can accomplish. Think about everything you want and make up a list of up to a hundred things.

If you spend just ten minutes with your goals every morning, it could take you weeks, until you get to the point where you feel that "yes, this is all I want." Write down not only what you want to have, but also—first of all—ways in which you want to *be*.

Life works like that: BE-DO-HAVE. (For example, I **am** disciplined - I'm **doing** my yoga every week - I **have** a healthy body and a clear mind.) Our goals are very important. My suggestion is to start your list of goals this way:

I invite God to take over and wipe away anything that is not aligned with my divine purpose, and give me even more blessings and soul missions, as I am his beloved child.

Write down long-term goals and short-term goals.

When you're done, continue to spend a few minutes every morning reading your list of goals. It will give you the big picture of your life. It will keep you in touch with who you really are and what you really want. You'll never get lost in the day-to-day problems. You'll see your life as you can see the land from the window of a plane.

Visualization: Based on your list of goals, make a collage with images and words that represent the big picture for who you want to be, and what you want to do and have. Look at it every day and imagine yourself in the way you want to be; imagine yourself in places you love. Add a picture of each person who you love. Look at their pictures and wish them the best in the world, from the bottom of your heart. This will keep you connected to them. You'll feel *one* with them.

———

You'll love them more, you'll care about them more, and you'll live in pure, genuine love with them. Your goals become your vision. Your day is already a success just by going through this process.

My collage

Affirmations: Program your mind. Give your mind instructions on how you want to *be*.

Pick three ways of being that you want for yourself. No more than three.

Write them down in the present tense (for example, "I am focused," or "I am calm").
If your affirmation is too far away from your actual belief of yourself, use the word "choose" (for example, "I choose to have a millionaire mind," or "I choose to be slim and in a perfect shape").

Do not use any negative words (for example, "I'm not fat," or "I don't smoke anymore").

Stay comfortable and relaxed while saying the affirmations aloud.
It is even more powerful to look into your own eyes in the mirror while saying them. It builds more confidence and generates more self-love.

Say each one twenty times—loud enough so that your ear will hear from the inside and from the outside. Feel the feeling of being that way, and visualize yourself acting upon being this way. Try to get rid of any other thoughts with calm and the acceptance that is normal to have other thoughts coming to you.

Keep doing your affirmations for ninety days. After ninety days, if you choose to continue, replace the ones that you feel now as being a part of you with other affirmations. Be patient with yourself.

Meditation: Quiet your mind for fifteen minutes every day. Connect with your inner being, where all the answers are. Breathe and focus on your breathing. Have joy and ease. Choose a meditation technique that most fits your personality. See the chapter below on "Meditations." Invent your own meditations, as you are inspired to do so.

Discipline is the bridge between goals and accomplishment.
—Jim Rohn, motivational speaker, author, and entrepreneur

———

B: A powerful way of living life

Get to a higher and higher degree of **Peace of Mind.**
Peace of mind means freedom from fear, anger, and guilt.

Letting go of fear: Fear comes from inside. It is a story
that has been cultivated and developed. Even if it is never
going to completely disappear, it can be diminished and
overcome by acting despite of it. It is essential that we
know that we are never alone. God is right here, for all of
us. God is love. When we know that, fear vanishes,
because fear can't exist in the same place as love.

Forgiveness and acceptance are the keys to freedom from
anger and guilt.

Forgiveness: To forgive means to let go of any negative
emotions. Only when you're able to send love do you
know you have completely forgiven, with thoughts and
feelings.

Acceptance: Acceptance means to be able to trust that
everything happens for a reason. It could be simply a step
on your path toward your greatness. Let go and feel free.
Accept yourself as you are, your deeds as they were,
things as they are, people as they are, without resisting
and feeling negative emotions.

Detachment: Our problems are most of the time only in
our head. Life is wonderful. Look at yourself from the
outside, and be your own observer. Have the big picture
of your life and of life itself. Set yourself free, and by
doing so you'll set everyone around you free.

Choose your thoughts: What you choose to think is what you attract and what you become. You can create your life, as you think with feelings. Practice choosing your thoughts carefully. They will still come and go, but don't develop any thought that doesn't serve you.

Believe: Believe what is best for you is what is going to happen. If anything bad still happens to you, its purpose is just to make you stronger and to teach you a lesson. Learn your lesson and move on.

Trust: Trust your inner voice—your intuition. Be open, expect to hear it, trust it, and act upon it.

Program your mind: Practice affirmations.

Be connected: Connect with the beauty and power of life, with nature, with yourself, and with people in your life.

Have discipline: Without discipline, nothing stays in good shape; moreover, nothing grows or blossoms.

Believe in miracles: Dream like a child. Go to sleep with something in mind that makes your soul vibrate. Everything that you are inspired to dream of, you can accomplish.

Give up self-limiting beliefs: Such as: "I can't be, do, or have that;" "I can only have five good friends;" "I can only have one great love in my life;" or "I was already lucky once, this would be too good to be true."

Live in love: Our ability to love has no limits. Love is the blood flowing through our veins. Love is the greatest power in the universe. Every second lived in love is invested. Every second lived without love is lost. When we don't love, we feel emptiness. When we don't love people thinking that they don't deserve our love, we feel powerless and empty.

Concentrate, focus: The best way you can help yourself get out of a bad situation is to focus on something that protects and supports you. The way you can create your most desirable experience is to focus on what you want. The way you can help yourself and others is to focus with intense desire, with no interruptions, on the positive energy that you want to let flow through you.

When you're down, remember who you really are. Put aside whatever bothers you and reconnect to your power within. Read a good book, listen to a CD, meditate, pray, call a good friend. The bad moment will go and then the whole context through which you see your "problem" will change. No one was always connected to the light within. Bad moments come to balance and sometimes are playing the role of a flu shot. Replace the ideas, beliefs, and emotions that create lack of power with new, supportive ideas that will give you a new perspective.

Remember, "You are powerful beyond measure."

We all need to help ourselves first, and by doing so we automatically help others, too—simply because we are all <u>*one*</u>*.*

Meditations

The ultimate purpose of meditation is to connect to our higher self. Going within, being aware of our light within, feeling it, and transforming it into a flowing fountain of life-giving water, this is the pathway to enlightenment. It's said that prayer is "talking to God," and meditation is "listening to God."

As we're meditating, we're opening the door to the Universal Consciousness, and by doing so, we practice *being one*, which is the ultimate goal of humanity.

Many of the things you can count don't count. Many of the things you can't count really count.—Albert Einstein

Meditation is one of those things that really count.

"How should I meditate?" one may ask. There are an infinite number of ways we can meditate. We unconsciously meditate every second in which we are present, in the Now.

The only wrong way to meditate is to not meditate.
—Wayne Dyer

There is active meditation—when our mind is engaged in a process of balancing and energizing the body-mind-spirit.

Examples of active meditation techniques are countless: yoga, qigong, tai chi, basically any sports, the four elements meditations described below, the practice of affirmations, and many more.

There is also quiet meditation—when our mind's activity slows down tremendously, and we give up control, letting ourselves be a pure channel of energy. Quiet meditation can be best practiced at the end of an active meditation. An example of quiet meditation is watching the clouds coming and going, while surrendering and letting go of any thought process.

About the body-mind-spirit connection during meditation

(All information provided below about the human body has been drawn from the sciences of anatomy and physiology)

The autonomic nervous system—regulated by the hypothalamus
- Sympathetic nervous system—when we are stressed, adrenaline is released by the adrenal glands, which leads to a "fight or flight" response.
- Parasympathetic nervous system—when we are relaxed, conserving our body's resources, it works with the vagus nerve, which controls the heart rate, the digestive process, the respiratory process, the liver, pancreas, stomach, spleen, intestines, genitals, and kidneys.

Meditation activates the parasympathetic nervous system.

Endocrine and chakra systems and the importance of meditation

These two systems are closely interconnected and, along with the nervous system, constitute the command board of human beings.

There are seven endocrine glands: adrenal, gonads, pancreas, thymus, thyroid, pituitary, and pineal.

And seven main chakras:
- Root, matching the vibration of the color red
- Sacral, matching the vibration of the color orange
- Solar plexus, matching the vibration of the color yellow
- Heart, matching the vibration of the color green
- Third eye, matching the vibration of the color purple
- Crown, matching the vibration of the color violet or white

The pituitary gland regulates the adrenal gland, the thyroid, human growth, sperm production, egg development, ovulation, testosterone production, skin pigmentation, milk production, anti-diuretic hormone, milk expression, and uterine contractions. Known to be the "master gland," the pituitary sits in the sella turcica of the sphenoid bone, and is the most protected gland in the body. The sphenoid bone looks like a butterfly or dove. The third eye chakra is connected with the pituitary gland.

Any meditation stimulates the third eye chakra's harmonious functionality, but especially visualization exercises.

For example, when we look at a beautiful rose for a few minutes, and then, with our eyes closed, we visualize the rose in every detail, that simple action has an incredible positive effect on the entire body-mind-spirit system.

The pituitary gland has its own master, the hypothalamus, which sends hormones and nerve impulses to the pituitary and pineal glands. The hypothalamus is also called the "pearl of the brain."

The pineal gland produces melatonin, and is in charge of circadian rhythms (sleep, eating, blood renewal, menstrual circles, and the whole body's cyclic renewal). It is connected to the crown chakra.

The endocrine glands in our brain produce endorphins (the painkiller hormone) and oxytocin (the love hormone).

Endorphins and oxytocin are not released while afraid. Therefore, endocrine glands are confirming that love and fear can't be together at the same time. I choose God's love.

The thyroid is in charge of growth development, and mental, physical and metabolic activities. It is connected with the throat chakra.

The thymus is a very important part of the immune system. It produces T-cells—our body's army—until puberty, and then it atrophies.
It is connected with the heart chakra. Therefore, receiving love in childhood is crucial for the foundation of a strong immune system.

The pancreas decreases blood glucose or increases blood glucose as needed. It is connected with the solar plexus chakra.

The spleen stores blood cells and destroys old red blood cells. It produces antibodies and is part of the immune system. A bio-energy worker's spleen is bigger. In traditional Chinese medicine, the spleen channel is the primary organ responsible for the production of chi. It is also connected with the solar plexus chakra.

The gonads (ovaries and testes) are connected with the sacral chakra.

The adrenal produces adrenaline (causing the "fight or flight" response) and steroid hormones. It is connected with the root chakra, the center of our life-force energy, which is in charge of safety and security.

Meditation balances all chakras, which are connected to the endocrine glands, and therefore, leads to the well-being of our entire body.

Electrical brain waves and states of consciousness
1. Beta—wakeful consciousness, mentally active, and aware of one's exterior surroundings. *Do yoga* for balance.
2. Alpha—awake but relaxed, synchronization between the right and left parts of the brain, relaxation, self-healing, creativity, meditation.
Do affirmations with emotional involvement. Focus on one point or thing. After a while, it can go into the next stage.

3. Theta—deep relaxation, unfocused attention, dreamlike awareness, sleep, collective subconscious, out-of-body experiences.
4. Delta—deep sleep or coma-like states.

***

Below are just a few meditation techniques that have been making my life more joyous, covering the connection with the four elements—air, earth, water, and fire.

The more we merge with nature through meditation techniques, and find ourselves in it, the more we can learn to love and understand each other.

Breathing light meditation

Notice the difference between just breathing and meditating or visualizing that you're breathing light. As you breathe light, you bring into your awareness the omnipresence of God.

Let the light fill all your body, until you visualize yourself as a light ball, radiating light around you. Enjoy the union with divine light. Know that you are *one* with the Creator. Know that you are now a source of light in the world.

There are infinitely more sources of light in the world, just like the stars out there in the universe. Imagine that you see them on the map, shining, sustaining the balance and well-being of the human kind.

The Pleiades

Feel the power of spiritual partnership, with the other sources of light.

Now visualize a web of light, connecting you with each and every other being, dream about meeting them in person one day.

Enjoy as long as you wish, and then come back to here and now.

Gem stone meditation

Once I was holding a gemstone a shaman gave me. It felt great, knowing that the gemstone had received many blessings. All of a sudden, I shifted my attention toward the energy of the stone, rather than toward the energy of the universe coming down through the top of my head. "This stone is magic," I told myself. What does that mean? Whatever we dare to dream....

I closed my eyes and imagined that the gemstone in my hand transformed itself into a seed of divine light, having amazing powers. The light started then to spread through my palms, fingers, forearm, arm, shoulders, neck, and torso, until all my body transformed into a shiny light bowl, a source of divine light. My whole vibration changed. I was in a trance. The magnificence of the visualization took my breath away.

Years later, I shared this meditation with my meditation group, and invited everyone to imagine that while being made of divine light, any wish they could make was being instantly fulfilled. So I asked them to make a wish, and visualize and feel the joy of having it fulfilled. The second step of the meditation was to give a gift, to make someone else's wish come true.

Through receiving and giving, the flow of light was activated powerfully. This is the essence of being a healer, a medium.

This became a beautiful and powerful meditation, born from nothing but imagination.

You can invent meditation techniques, too. No matter how simple or sophisticated, they'll have the effect of shifting your vibration, of lowering the frequencies of the brain waves, and making room for spiritual miracles to unfold.

Shower meditation

While in the shower, one day I let the water fall straight on to my crown and I suddenly remembered Dr. Mikao Usui's experience of receiving the gift of enlightenment, the reiki powers, while meditating under a waterfall. Inspiration to search awakened in me. Moving my body slowly, I found the soft spot on the top of my head. It felt different as the water was falling there. I started to chant "Om," as in yoga, and the sound got louder. Keeping my hands right in front of my face, the sound came back to me even louder.

I was so present. The "Om" sounded louder and louder…. The shower seemed to transform into a shower of light.

I was taking a shower of divine light. We could always imagine that, just as we can always imagine that we're breathing light. "Om-ing" in the shower is a powerful experience you might love to try.

Each time we bring to routine activities an awareness of "now," we raise our vibratory frequency and cause the freshness of the moment to fall upon us.
—Rev. Dr. Michael Bernard Beckwith

Candle meditation

Once I was watching a lit candle, placed on top of a piece of furniture. Right underneath was a picture of Jesus. At some point, the candle melted and wax was dripping down over Jesus' face. Instantly, I felt a message deep in my heart: "Pray to Jesus while you're gazing into the candle." This was a message for me, as Jesus is my master guide. A message for you could be to pray to your master guide. The whole point is to connect with the divine powers.

Gazing into the flame of a candle brings so much peace. Whenever you feel angry, disconnected from the Source, confused, stressed, or sad, take a candle and place it somewhere you can watch it right in front of your eyes, if possible in a dark room. Light the candle and gaze into the flame for a while. Feel the light of the candle nurturing your soul. Feel the darkness leaving you, and let the light in. More and more, you will find peace. The mind chatter will be replaced by silence, or, sometimes, by a very meaningful message for you, provided by your higher self, or by the divine help we all have.

Knowing that candle meditation is an open gate for divine help you can ask questions, while looking at the simple, basic, but so magical flame. Your breathing will slow down, and your mind will become more and more quiet. Then, imagine that the light is in your heart. You become a source of peace, harmony, and love. Enjoy the feeling.

Candle meditation

Now think about one person in your life that you would like to share peace with. Imagine that you're having the candle's flame in your hand, and you're offering it to that person. You are placing the light in their heart. You see the light in their heart. You see them lighting up with peace and love. You are connected to each other through unconditional love.

Enjoy the feeling as long as you want.

Close your eyes for a few minutes and keep watching the candle, inside of you.

You can expand this meditation in many ways. Whatever comes to mind is what you're called to do. Follow the joy of your creation.

When you are ready, come back to here and now.

Meditation on the beach

Sit comfortably in lotus posture, with your spine straight.
Close your eyes and imagine that you are on a wonderful
beach. The *water* is turquoise blue. The *sky* is blue, too,
and just a few white clouds are crossing it. The sand is
white and warm under your feet. You are walking down
the beach, and you can feel the warm, soft *sand* under
your feet. You are taking a deep breath, filling your lungs
with fresh air, while hearing the waves and the birds.
Your thoughts are coming and going, just like the clouds
on the sky. You are more and more detached.

Looking down, you see little shells and colorful stones in
the sand. You pick up a few, enjoying their shapes and
colors. *You are finding precious gifts in infinity.*

The ocean is on your right.

As you look on your left, you see a garden of *red* roses.
Step inside and go into the middle of it.

Surround yourself with red roses. Look at their petals, touch them, smell them, enjoy the vibrant color, and imagine that you are one of them—a beautiful, red rose. Breathe in and out a few times, inhaling the red, vibrant color.

Say to yourself: *I am safe. I am centered. I am grounded and connected to the earth. I am filled with life-force energy.*

Then, come outside and feel the warm and soft sand under your feet again. Hear the waves. Let them go over your ankles. Feel the breeze, and then keep walking again.

As you look on your left, you see a garden of *orange* roses. Step inside and go into the middle of it. Surround yourself with orange roses. Look at their petals, touch them, smell them, enjoy the vibrant color, and imagine that you are one of them—a beautiful, orange rose. Breathe in and out a few times, inhaling the orange, vibrant color.

Say to yourself: *I am passionate. I am connected with my dear ones. I let things flow.*

Then, come outside and feel the warm and soft sand under your feet again. Hear the waves. Let them go over your ankles. Feel the breeze, and then keep walking again.

As you look on your left, you see a garden of *yellow* roses. Step inside and go into the middle of it. Surround yourself with yellow roses.

Look at their petals, touch them, smell them, enjoy the vibrant color, and imagine that you are one of them—a beautiful, yellow rose. Breathe in and out a few times, inhaling the yellow, vibrant color.

Say to yourself: *I stand in my power. I am disciplined. I am joyful and committed to my goals. I can accomplish everything I want.*

Then, come outside and feel the warm and soft sand under your feet again. Hear the waves. Let them go over your ankles. Feel the breeze, and then keep walking again.

As you look on your left, you see a field of fresh cut *green* grass. Step inside and go into the middle of it. Lie down and take a deep breath. Feel the freedom and infinity of your soul. Smell the green grass, and imagine that you are one with it. Breathe in and out a few times, inhaling the green, vibrant color.

Say to yourself: *I love myself. I can truly love. I am love.*

Feel your connection with everyone in your life, and know that you are not alone.

Then, slowly get up and come outside and feel the warm and soft sand under your feet again. Hear the waves. Let them go over your ankles. Feel the breeze....

And focus on the horizon line. Soften your eyes, gaze into the infinity of the *blue-turquoise* color of the ocean and the sky.

Imagine you are one with the sky, one with the ocean, omnipresent, powerful, infinite, connected with life, connected with all beings that breathe and contain water in their bodies … and feel the infinite power of your soul. Breathe in and out a few times, inhaling the blue, vibrant color.

Say to yourself: *I am self-expressed. I am confident in my communication—my speaking, my writing, and my listening.*

Feel the freedom and power of self-expression. Feel the connection through communication with everyone in your life. Through words, we can create.

Then, bring your focus back to the warm and soft sand under your feet. Hear the waves. Let them go over your ankles. Feel the breeze, and then keep walking again.

As you look on your left, you see a garden of *purple* wild flowers. Step inside and go into the middle of it. Surround yourself with purple, little flowers, look at their small petals, touch them, smell them, enjoy the vibrant color, and imagine that you are one of them—a beautiful, purple flower. Place one of them on your forehead, and imagine that the flower is the eye of your mind, your third eye. Imagine that, through the purple flower, you can see beyond any limits. Breath in and out a few times, inhaling the purple, vibrant color.

Say to yourself: *I am intuitive. I am a visionary. I am open to being psychic. I am a whole person enjoying my sixth sense.*

Imagine the freedom of always knowing the truth, being able to make the best decisions.

Then, come outside and feel the warm, soft sand under your feet again. Hear the waves. Let them go over your ankles. Feel the breeze, and then begin walking again.

As you look to your left, you see a lake filled with blossomed *white* lotuses. The flowers are big and bright, their petals are soft and shiny. Sit on the edge of the lake, and look at their petals. You can reach a lotus and touch it, smell it, enjoy the purity of it. Imagine that a ray of white divine light is coming down on to the blossomed lotus, transforming it into a radiant magical flower. Imagine that you are the lotus. Breathe in and out a few times, inhaling the white divine light.

Say to yourself: *I am one with the Creator; I am* one *with all that is.*

Feel your own infinity. Radiate with light. Feel your wholeness. Breathe deeply.

Then, come outside and feel the warm, soft sand under your feet again. Hear the waves. Let them go over your ankles. Feel the breeze, and then find a place to sit on the sand. Crystals are shining in the sand.

Right in front of you, there is a *fire* pit. Light the fire and observe the dance of its flames for a few minutes. Connect with its power. Then, close your eyes and keep observing the flame with the eyes of your mind.

By now, the daylight fades away, allowing you to see billions of stars in the sky.

You are connected with the whole universe. You are at peace, you are in bliss, and the healing energy of the universe surrounds you and flows through you.

Trust that life is an amazing gift and let the light flow through you.

There are colorful stars in the universe. There is so much healing energy in the universe, coming down in the form of colorful stars. There are colorful stars inside of us— our chakras. There are so many shiny stars in the world, just like us, forming a web of light. There are so many spiritual guides around us, showing themselves in the form of shiny stars. All these colorful stars are on an infinite journey, one of love, healing, and oneness. They are here for us. They are one *with us.*

Focus on your breathing, and go deep within. Feel the bliss even more. Quiet your mind and keep breathing. Allow yourself to *just be.*

When you are ready, slowly come back to here and now.

***

I am grateful, humbled, and joyful.
Thank you, Creator.
Thank you masters, healers, and teachers.
Thank you, soul-family.
Thank you, open hearts.
Let's keep traveling together.
We are on the journey of the colorful stars!

About the Author

Laura O'Neale is a Reiki Master/Teacher, Certified Massage Therapist and Meditation Techniques Guide. Her soul mission is to heal and teach through spiritual love. She knows that we are all beloved children of the Universe, and she has been called to assist the seekers toward their happiness.

Laura earned a Bachelors Degree in Computer Science in Romania, her home country. Currently, she resides in Washington, D.C. However, she considers herself a universal soul, because people around the world have a home in her heart.

Please visit Laura at www.YourLightWithin.com

Laura's books:

The Journey of the Colorful Stars
A Pathway toward Love, Faith, and Healing

&

Reiki and the Path to Enlightenment
A Reiki and Shamanic Journal for Energy Healing Students, Practitioners, and Teachers

&

Focused on Spirit
A Journal about Spiritual Gifts Serving Humanity

www.ingramcontent.com/pod-product-compliance
Lightning Source LLC
Chambersburg PA
CBHW060936040426
42445CB00011B/893